ABSINTHE

BARNABY CONRAD III

ABSINTHE

HISTORY IN A BOTTLE

CHRONICLE BOOKS

SAN FRANCISCO

Grateful acknowledgement is made for permission to reprint:

Harry Crosby, quoted from *Shadows of the Sun*. Copyright © 1977 Edward Germain and Black Sparrow Press.

Ernest Hemingway, quoted from *The Sun Also Rises*. Copyright © 1926 Charles Scribner's Sons; copyright renewed © 1954 Ernest Hemingway. Reprinted with the permission of Charles Scribner's Sons, Jonathan Cape Ltd., and the Executors of the Estate of Ernest Hemingway.

Ernest Hemingway, quoted from *For Whom the Bell Tolls*. Copyright © 1940 Ernest Hemingway; copyright renewed © 1968 Mary Hemingway. Reprinted with the permission of Charles Scribner's Sons, Jonathan Cape Ltd., and the Executors of the Estate of Ernest Hemingway.

Ernest Hemingway, quoted from *Death in the Afternoon*. Copyright © 1932 Charles Scribner's Sons; copyright renewed © 1960 Ernest Hemingway. Reprinted with the permission of Charles Scribner's Sons, Jonathan Cape Ltd., and the Executors of the Estate of Ernest Hemingway.

Printed in Hong Kong.

Library of Congress Cataloging-in-Publication Data available.

ISBN 0-8118-1650-8

Editing: Charles Robbins
Cover Design: Jane Elizabeth Brown
Book Design: Steve Renick
Front Cover: *The Absinthe Drinkers*, by Jean François Raffaëlli
Back Cover: Absinthe Suisse label
Composition: Dharma Enterprises

Distributed in Canada by
Raincoast Books
8680 Cambie Street
Vancouver, B.C. V6P 6M9

10 9 8 7 6 5 4 3

Chronicle Books
85 Second Street
San Francisco, CA 94105

www.chroniclebooks.com

Contents

Acknowledgements

I would like to thank Nion McEvoy, Bill LeBlond, and Chuck Robbins for editing the book; Steve Renick for designing it; Marie-Claude Delahaye for her inspiration; Myron Kunin, Joseph H. Hazen, Heinz Berggruen, Raymond Klein, Mrs. Melville W. Hall, Max Rutherston, and Joël Guiraud at the Musée de Pontarlier for generously loaning their art; Manuel Burrus and Mark Potter for their photo research; Wiley Wood for his translations; Marie-France Briselance and Jean-Marc Andrié of Pernod, S.A.; Ronald K. Siegel and Ada E. Hirschman for their material on Henri Balesta; Georges Bernier, Michael Albert-Puleo, Robert Noecker, John Bellamy Taylor, Maurie Neville, Bruce Schroffel, Roger Knights, David Graves, Michael Montagne, and my father, B.C., Jr., for their absinthiana; Madame Alemany-Dessaint of the Musée du Louvre and Madame Lernaut of the Musée de Picardie, Amiens for finding the Maignan picture; Roland de L'Espée and Marie de la Chevardiere; Martin Muller for his bottle of absinthe; John and Gretchen Berggruen for their support; John Martin of Black Sparrow Press; Laura Miller of Colorarts and Betsey Bourbon and Christina Yoder of Skylab; Mary Bersot, Walter Lees, Madeleine Lesne, Duncan Chapman, John Crichton, Milly de Surian, Taki, and Geri Hughes for their generosity; Pierre and Nicole Schwarz for their kindness to a stranger; and my agent Michael Congdon.

For My Mother   DALE CRICHTON

Who brought you into the world, and ever since,

    a tender mother,

Standing you double stead in this bitter life,

Has always drunk the absinthe and left the

    honey for you.

(Victor Hugo)

Introduction

nineteenth-century novelist, Prosper Méri-mée, once said that what he liked in history were anecdotes, "and among anecdotes I prefer those where I think that I can distinguish a true picture of the customs and characters of any given period." Nineteenth-century France was full of anecdotes about a peculiar drink that touched almost every aspect of its culture: Absinthe.

Take the story of poet Alfred de Musset, one of the greatest men of letters France produced in the first half of the last century. He wrote his first brilliant work as a teenager in 1829, and at thirty-one he was admitted to the august body of the Académie française. Yet from then on, he wrote almost no poetry and frequently missed the dictionary sessions at the Academy. When it was brought to the attention of Abel François Ville-main, secretary of the Academy, that Musset "s'absent souvent" (is often absent), he replied sourly, "Vous voulez dire qu'il s'absinthe un peu trop." (You mean to say that he *absinthes* a little too much) — and a new verb was born within the Academy, that sacred fortress of the French language. Indeed, like many of his generation, Mus-set absinthe-ed too much, dying at an unusually early age.

By the turn of the century, five o'clock in the afternoon saw the cafés on the grand boulevards of Paris filled with smartly dressed men and women taking a moment to drink the milky, opalescent beverage and watch life go by. Ab-sinthe was familiarly known as "La Fée Verte" or the Green Fairy, and so popular did it become that cocktail hour was known as l'heure verte after absinthe's pale emerald hue.

One of Oscar Wilde's biographers, R.H. Sher-ard, tells an anecdote about a heavy absinthe drinker who was ashamed to be seen lingering at the same café too long: "He takes his first drink at one café, his second somewhere else, and his tenth or twelfth at some tenth or twelfth other café. I know a very distinguished musician who used to start off at the Café Napolitan and finish up at the Gare du Nord." It sets the mind thinking about the cafés of Paris, of the brilliance that flashed and wasted itself there.

What were the effects of absinthe? Oscar Wilde, who had a taste for absinthe, gave his impressions to John Fothergill, who recorded it in his book, *My Three Inns:*

"The first stage is like ordinary drinking, the second when you begin to see monstrous and cruel things, but if you can persevere you will enter in upon the third stage where you see things that you *want* to see, wonderful curious things. One night I was left sitting, drinking alone, and very late in the Café Royal, and I had just got into the third stage when a waiter came in with a green apron and began to pile the chairs on the tables. 'Time to go, sir,' he called to me. Then he brought in a watering can and began to water the floor. 'Time's up, sir. I'm afraid you must go now, sir.'

"'Waiter, are you watering the flowers?' I asked but he didn't answer.

"'What are your favorite flowers, waiter?' I asked again. 'Now, sir, I must really ask you to go now, time's up,' he said firmly. 'I'm sure that tulips are your favorite flowers,' I said, and as I got up and passed out into the street I felt — the — heavy — tulip — heads — brushing against my shins."

I particularly like this vignette which indicates how ubiquitous a custom absinthe was: Once in the Ghent railroad station, the most famous absinthe drinker of all, Paul Verlaine, encountered the Belgian dramatist Maurice Maeterlinck, who had haunted the cafés of Paris as a young law student. Although Maeterlinck didn't know the older poet well, he had admired his poetry and recognized Verlaine easily enough: "The Brussels train came to a halt in the almost deserted station. A window in a third class carriage opened with a great clatter and framed the faun-like face of the old poet. 'I take sugar with it!' he cried. This was apparently his usual greeting when he was on his travels: a sort of war-cry or password, which meant that he took sugar with his absinthe."

Absinthe enjoyed a vogue around the world from Vienna to New York. In 1893, Maurice Barrymore, father of John, Ethel, and Lionel, the "royal family of the theater," presented a bottle of absinthe to his friend, Thomas G. Patten, the prominent banker, at his Eighteenth Street mansion. Patten's stepdaughter, Mamie Floyd, insisted upon tasting it. "It is like something I had when I was a child," she said, wrinkling up her nose. "I mean it's just like paregoric."

"You're quite right," Barrymore laughed. "Absinthe is the paregoric of second childhood."

In Paris, the Goncourt brothers, Edmond and Jules, made their famous journal the repository for a century's details and a number relate to absinthe. For example, in January 1891, Edmond (who carried on the journal after Jules died in 1870)

Alfred de Musset, whose literary ambitions were dulled by absinthe.

Paul Verlaine in an absinthe reverie.

Actor Maurice Barrymore once called absinthe "the paregoric of second childhood."

recorded this dreadful little portrait in miniature of a seedy boarding house and how absinthe ruined two lives: "An old society woman, *une absintheuse*, who soaked up 22 absinthes a day, of that awful absinthe colored with zinc sulphate . . . a sexagenarian whose lawyer son never knew how to get her out of there and who, according to the legend of the neighborhood, was killed by despair and shame. . . ."

Now *that* is a story that tells you something about the habits and shattered hopes of an age. Imagine drinking twenty-two glasses of anything, much less a drink like absinthe which was 72 percent alcohol.

Then there was the poet Théodore Pelloquet who never found consistent work as satisfying as the pleasure of conversation and absinthe at a café called Dinochau's. His habits took him to the edge of insanity. It is said that as he lay dying in Nice, he struggled to say some word but could only stutter the first syllable: "Abs . . . abs . . . ." Those around him thought he was asking for absolution until he finally wheezed: "Absinthe."

These slices of social life make absinthe sound like a terrible, addictive poison — and that is its reputation today. Yet for millions of Frenchmen who drank it in moderation, absinthe was little more than a pleasant, refreshing drink.

By the fin de siècle, alcoholism was a growing problem in France, but it was not well understood. For the anti-alcoholic movement, the glass of green absinthe shimmering on a café table symbolized anarchy, a deliberate denial of normal life and its obligations. By 1914, politicians, generals, doctors, and temperance zealots developed the momentum to ban absinthe.

Even in its last days, we find an anecdote that illustrates absinthe's hold on the French consciousness. While trying to defend absinthe in the French Chamber of Deputies, Adolphe Girod pointed out to the anti-alcohol bloc how ridiculous it was to endanger a great industry with heavy taxes or banishment. Making little headway using traditional methods, Girod grew so desperate, he appealed to the politicians' aesthetic sense. "For God's sake," he cried, "at least absinthe has inspired such beautiful poems by Alfred de Musset!"

Buveurs d'Absinthe, by an anonymous artist of the 1870s.

Edmond de Goncourt confessed in a journal entry of September 1885: "And by God, I have put myself on a diet so that if, say, we have an absinthe, we have it with laudanum."

Even such gallant words could not save the Green Fairy as France entered the Great War. The drink that inspired poets and artists was forgotten as a million and half French soldiers died in the trenches.

I began collecting these anecdotes some ten years ago and have come to see absinthe as a skeleton key to the fin de siècle's secrets. And though there are some pleasant anecdotes, the history of absinthe also holds murder, madness, and despair. So, yes, you would do well to take it as Verlaine did, with some sugar.

An absinthe drinker by Neuchâtel artist
Daniel Ihly (1902). Note the cork in the
man's mouth.

Chapter 1

An Absinthe Murder

On the yellow dawn of August 28, 1905, while his wife and children slept, Jean Lanfray rose and dressed in the second-floor bedroom of his family's dilapidated farmhouse in Commugny, a small village within the French-speaking canton of Vaud, Switzerland. As was his habit before work, the thirty-one-year-old laborer poured himself a shot of absinthe, lightly diluted with water. Lanfray liked the pale green color and the strong anise flavor, refreshing and stringent enough to remove the taste of last night's wine.

Downstairs in the kitchen, he found his brother and father stirring. Lanfray was pouring himself a second absinthe and water when his wife came down to cook breakfast. Since he planned to gather mushrooms in the woods the next day, Lanfray told her to wax his boots. When she shrugged, he repeated the order harshly and then went out to tend the cows. A big, burly Frenchman who had soldiered for three years with the Chasseurs Alpins, Lanfray was given to shouting at his wife from time to time. But he wasn't a bad fellow, the villagers would say later, not the type you'd think capable of murder . . . even after drinking absinthe.

Lanfray, his brother, and father had bread and coffee and then left the house. It was 5:30 A.M. when they stopped off at the local café. There were others bolstering themselves with coffee and cheap brandies before a day in the vineyards. Lanfray downed a crème de menthe and then ordered a cognac and soda. He watched as another worker asked for an absinthe. The barman set the tall glass on the zinc counter for the ritual preparation. From a bottle, he poured an inch of pale green liquor into the glass. The barman let his customers do their own mixing. The worker placed a lump of sugar on a perforated trowel and balanced it over the glass. Then he poured water slowly over the sugar which disintegrated and dripped into the glass below, clouding the absinthe to a milky green.

Lanfray himself might have considered ordering an absinthe, but as it was late, he finished his cigarette and headed to the vineyards. It turned into a hot, muggy day, so during lunch and an afternoon wine break he put away a total of six glasses of *piquette*, the heady local wine. At 4:15 Lanfray drank another glass of wine. At 4:30 they quit work and walked to a little café near the vineyards where Lanfray drank a cup of coffee laced with brandy.

One eye on the absinthe glass. A water-color from the 1870s.

That evening, Lanfray stepped into his farm-house and rudely banged the door shut behind him. His wife frowned at her husband's behavior and glazed eyes, shook her head with disgust, and went back to her needlework. Sitting at the kitch-en table, Lanfray and his father each polished off another liter of *piquette*.

Lanfray's wife asked him to milk the cows. He told her to milk the cows herself. Lanfray poured himself some coffee and laced it with a big slug of *marc*, the powerful brandy he made himself. Then

he saw his boots sitting under the sink. They were still unwaxed. He turned on his wife, and the tiff escalated to shouting. When she accused him and his father of laziness, Lanfray lashed out, demand-ing she show respect for her elders. She yelled back. Shut up, he commanded. Try to make me, she answered.

Without a word more, Lanfray snatched his army rifle from a closet. The Vetterli was a long-barreled, bolt-action repeater with a magazine that held twelve cartridges. As his horrified father watched from the doorway, Lanfray aimed the rifle at his wife's face and fired. The bullet zipped through her forehead just above the right eye and exited her skull with spectacular effect. She fell dead near the hearthstone.

The old man fled out the front door. From the back of the house, Lanfray's four-and-a-half-year-old daughter Rose appeared in the doorway, star-ing at her mother's fallen form. Without hesitation Lanfray shot her in the chest, and she fell mortally wounded on the stone floor. Lanfray stepped across her body, went into the next room, and shot his two-year-old daughter Blanche who lay in a crib.

Lanfray now pressed the muzzle of the gun to his own sweating brow, but the Vetterli's thirty-inch barrel made it impossible for him to reach the trigger. In his frenzy, he tied a piece of string to the trigger and drew it behind the trigger guard for leverage. It was an unwieldy rig and the trigger was stiff. He jerked the string and the gun fired, blowing him backwards against the table. His unsteady aim had sent the bullet into his jawbone. Bleeding profusely but in no danger of dying, Lanfray dropped the gun, lifted the corpse of his infant daughter from the blood-soaked cradle, and stumbled outside. He crossed the courtyard to the barn where he collapsed into a deep sleep, clutch-ing the dead baby in his arms.

Lanfray's father arrived a few minutes later with the police. They carried Lanfray semi-conscious to the infirmary at Nyon where the bullet was extracted from his jaw. A few hours later, emerging from a daze, Lanfray was taken to see the bodies of his family. They lay in pathetic coffins of descending sizes. A nurse, Marie Blaser, recalled that the murderer pressed his fingers to his eyes and whimpered over and over, "Please, oh, God, please tell me I haven't done this. I loved my wife and children so much!"

A week later, in a Sunday meeting at the local schoolhouse, the citizens of Commugny learned that at the time of her death Madame Lanfray had

L'HEURE VERTE

— La vuitième, j'y mets toujours ed' l'eau.

In this 1897 anti-absinthe cartoon, the slurring drunk says, "I always add a li'l water to th'eighth glass."

been four months pregnant with a male fetus. An intense police inquiry began into Lanfray's drinking habits. It was learned that he sometimes downed up to five liters of wine a day. It was considered significant that on the day of the murder, Lanfray had drunk not just wine and brandy, but two large glasses of absinthe. Some of the authorities took grim pleasure in hearing this. "Un absinthiste!" cried the newspaper headlines.

The story of the "absinthe murder" hit the front page of most newspapers in Europe. Within a matter of weeks, a petition was signed by 34,375 men and 48,075 women (almost a third of the canton of Vaud's population) which demanded the immediate ban of absinthe in the canton. The number of women — who as yet had no right to vote — is significant and was no doubt due to Madame Lanfray's pregnant state.

La Gazette de Lausanne covered all the developments of the anti-absinthe movement and called absinthe "the premier cause of bloodthirsty crime in this country." The fact that Lanfray had consumed liter after liter of strong wine and numerous other cocktails was conveniently forgotten at the mention of two glasses of absinthe.

In detention, while awaiting sentencing, Lanfray was "calm, submissive, and discreet," spending his time embroidering little silken ornaments with remarkable skill.

In the highly publicized trial of February 23, 1906, Lanfray's lawyers maintained that the defendant was not mentally responsible for the crime because of his intoxicated state. The leading Swiss psychiatrist of the time, Dr. Albert Mahaim, who had observed Lanfray in the institution at Cery, testified that Lanfray suffered from a classic case of absinthe madness. "Without a doubt, it is the absinthe he drank daily and for a long time that gave Lanfray the ferociousness of temper and blind rages that made him shoot his wife for nothing and his two poor children, whom he loved."

The prosecutor, Alfred Obrist, disagreed. Lanfray had only ingested two ounces of absinthe in the ten hours before the murder along with much larger amounts of wine and cordials. The two absinthes, maintained the prosecution, were minor in relation to his habitual daily intake of wine. As the academics split hairs over absinthe's role in his mental state, Jean Lanfray was convicted of quadruple murder and was sentenced to thirty years imprisonment. Three days later he hung himself in his cell.

Lanfray's trial was over, but absinthe's was just beginning. On May 15, 1906, the Vaud legislature voted to ban the Green Fairy, and soon debates about this popular drink rose to a national level. From bars and bedrooms to newspaper offices and government chambers, the people of Switzerland were talking about absinthe.

A few days after Lanfray murdered his family, an equally gory incident had shocked the residents of Geneva. A man named Sallaz, who lived in the Rue de la Pelisserie, came off an absinthe binge and, with a burst of malevolent gusto, used a hatchet and revolver to murder his wife. Geneva followed the procedure taken by the canton of Vaud, and by January 1906, an anti-absinthe petition had gathered 34,702 signatures.

The Swiss government named a commission of experts including Dr. Albert Mahaim, Dr. César Roux, and Dr. Marc Dufour to study the drink and its effect. Their deliberation was brief, and their report strongly condemned the liquor.

For absinthe producers this was bad news. Though their main market was France, Switzerland was also very important. Second only to Vaud, Geneva consumed the most absinthe of any canton in Switzerland — 500,000 litres for 150,000 inhabitants, or three liters per capita per year. The pro-alcoholic bloc mobilized, fearing that if absinthe were outlawed, it would not be long before *all* alcoholic drinks were banned. Café and cabaret owners — supported by the distilleries — organized a lobby and roused support among their drinking clientele.

Some politicians began urging half-way measures: requiring café owners to buy a special license to sell absinthe or even letting the state run a monopoly on the fabrication, presumably, with government regulation, a higher grade of absinthe and therefore a healthier product would result. "This would make the State an entrepreneur of immorality," shouted Henri Hayem before the Swiss Chamber of Deputies in June 1906. "Why doesn't it also get a monopoly on prostitution? What's the difference?"

Why all the fuss over a drink? Because absinthe was big business. The Pernod family and other name brands such as Cusenier and Duval had turned a folk recipe for absinthe into an enormous multi-million franc industry with Switzerland alone exporting 3,000,000 gallons. Under pressure from café owners and manufacturers, a popular vote was held in Geneva, but again absinthe lost, 23,062 to 16,025. The producers continued to protest on the grounds that a ban would infringe on the liberty of commerce and industry, rights very dear to the Swiss. Yet in a growing fervor among medical groups and temperance leagues, absinthe was being cornered.

On February 2, 1907, the Grand Conseil voted to ban the retail sale of absinthe — and even its imitations — and this was ratified by popular vote. A year later, on July 5, 1908, by popular vote of 241,078 to 139,699, article 32 was added to the federal constitution, and absinthe was forbidden in Switzerland. The law went into effect October 7, 1910. The next day, *La Gazette de Lausanne* proudly noted that in banning the Green Fairy, "The Swiss people have shown their self-discipline, their sense of true liberty, and their moral vigor."

Actually, Switzerland wasn't the first country to ban absinthe. Belgium had quietly outlawed absinthe in 1905. Holland followed in 1910, and in

Switzerland banned absinthe in 1908, and it became law on October 7, 1910. The demonic preacher with the blue cross represents the temperance league conquering La Fée Verte, the Green Fairy.

1912 even the United States declared it illegal. A certain Mr. Wiley of the U.S. Pure Food Board declared that absinthe was "one of the worst enemies of man, and if we can keep the people of the United States from becoming slaves to this demon, we will do it."

In the early years of the twentieth century, anti-alcoholic movements flourished in Europe: Iceland banned all wines and spirits from 1908 to 1934, followed by Russia (1914 to 1924), Norway (1916 to 1927), and Finland (1919 to 1932). And the United States banned all alcohol from 1920 to 1933. But no individiual alcoholic drink except absinthe has ever been singled out for prohibition. Around the world, absinthe was banished before

Absinthe Mugnier of Dijon and Geneva promoted its product with a French soldier known as a "Zouave."

World War I — everywhere except England, Spain, and France. The English never really developed a taste for it, and in Spain absinthe consumption was relatively low. But in France, absinthe continued to be drunk with undiminished enthusiasm right up until the First World War.

Though invented by the Swiss, absinthe has always been associated with the French. The age of absinthe began in the 1840s during the Algerian War when French soldiers were issued absinthe as a fever preventative. When they returned to France, they brought the taste for absinthe with them. In 1912, the French drank 221,897,000 liters of absinthe a year, so much that society columnist Alfred Capus declared, "Absinthe has become the favorite drink of almost every French man."

Yet soon, even in Paris, the cry was raised against the Green Fairy. The clergy, politicians, and doctors blamed it for all the ills of a faltering nation. Denunciations reached such a pitch that an outspoken member of the French anti-alcoholic league, literary man Georges Ohnet, could declare in 1907, "If absinthe isn't banned, our country will rapidly become an immense padded cell where half the Frenchmen will be occupied putting straight jackets on the other half." The fact that absinthe accounted for only 3 percent of all the alcoholic beverages consumed (including wine) demonstrates how hysterical this debate became.

But let's not talk about absinthe's demise too soon. Imagine you have taken a table at the Café de la Paix, once a favorite rendezvous for Edouard Manet and the other impressionist painters. It is early evening, and you have all the time in the world to watch the carriages rattling up the Boulevard des Italiens toward the recently constructed Opéra. A waiter with a waxed moustache and fresh linen apron comes by to take your order: "L'Absinthe, s'il vous plaît."

With the first sip of the tongue-numbing, stomach-warming, idea-changing green drink, you forget about all that unpleasantness — the murder in Switzerland, the squabbling politicians, the doctors with their inconclusive experiments. With a well-sugared absinthe sitting before you on the marble tabletop, you have a chance at understanding what the poet-inventor Charles Cros meant when he wrote, "Absinthe, on a winter evening, / Lights up in green the sooty soul."

The abuses of wine absinthe are cleverly
illustrated in this engraving by Morin.

Café patrons drinking absinthe. One
observer wrote: "Paris has only 17,000
bakers, 14,500 butchers, but 33,000
drinksellers."

The Absinthe Drinker, 1859, by
Edouard Manet.

Chapter 2

Manet, Baudelaire, and the Absinthe Era

In the winter of 1859, twenty-six-year-old Edouard Manet finished a nearly life-size portrait of a street bum and titled it *The Absinthe Drinker*. The canvas had a pictorial grandeur more suitable for a duke than for a drunken ragpicker sporting a battered top hat. The man's grubby face bears an expression that is both defiant and contemplative. His left foot thrusts forward as if he were about to step into a light-headed jig, and beside him sits a gleaming glass of emerald absinthe.

Artists had painted drinkers for centuries, and paintings with drinking subjects were regularly accepted at the annual Salon of Paris. But when *The Absinthe Drinker* was presented to the selection committee of the 1859 Salon, it was summarily rejected. Why?

Part of the answer lies in the subject matter — absinthe was a new "industrial" drink replacing the traditional wine on the terraces of fashionable cafés. But it also had something to do with the detached, almost clinical way Manet presents his subject. There is no passion for the heroic, no storytelling warmth, and no clear moral viewpoint. Life is as it is. There is a clumsy, dark power to *The Absinthe Drinker*, echoing the words of the great poet Charles Baudelaire: "One must be drunk always. . . . If you would not feel the hor-

rible burden of Time that breaks your shoulders and bows you to the earth, you must intoxicate yourself unceasingly. But with what? With wine, poetry, or with virtue, your choice. But intoxicate yourself."

The rest of the answer lies in the climate of the times. After Napoléon I's resounding loss at Waterloo in 1815, France suffered a gradual decline. Under the reign of the "citizen king" Louis-Philippe (1830 to 1848), the bourgeoisie flourished along with industrialization, while revolutionary ideals replaced time-honored notions of patriotism and religion. During the political turmoil of 1848, Louis-Napoléon Bonaparte, nephew of the emperor, came out of exile and was elected president of the republic. Just three years later, he declared himself emperor. Under Napoléon III, industrialization changed centuries-old social relationships and attracted thousands of workers to Paris. The wrecking ball of Baron Haussmann, gaslighting, and railroads brought "progress" to medieval Paris.

Understandably, during this time, the best bourgeois precepts reigned supreme, and art of any originality had a hard time being accepted. "France," Baudelaire wrote in 1861, "is passing through a period of vulgarity. Paris is a center

Louis-Napoléon Bonaparte, who reigned as Napoléon III from 1852 to 1871. He was so angered by "vulgar realism" that he once struck a painting by Courbet with his riding crop.

radiating universal stupidity." The aesthetic order of the day called for well-painted schmalz with nymphs, goddesses, and war heroes by the square meter, or genre paintings that sugarcoated the unhappy peasants and striking workers. Napoléon III is said to have walked through the Salon of 1853 and smacked a painting by Courbet with his riding crop, cursing its "vulgar realism."

Charles Baudelaire's earliest obsessions were literature and art. He spent hours in the Louvre looking at El Greco. A superb draughtsman himself, he worshipped the Romantic canvases of Delacroix. His book, *The Painter of Modern Life* (1863), had the greatest effect on the immediate generation of young painters, but as early as 1845 Baudelaire had challenged: "The *painter*, the true painter, will be he who can extract from present-day life its epic quality, and make us see and understand, through color and line, how great and poetic we are in our cravats and patent-leather boots."

He asked for an urban art, not the dreamy landscapes of the Barbizon School and said that high fashion and the sinister Parisian underworld of criminals and whores offered a kind of over-looked beauty — a conjecture that foreshadowed the rest of the century's art and poetry, from the whores of Lautrec to the alcoholics of Zola.

Baudelaire met Manet in 1858, the year before Manet painted *The Absinthe Drinker*, and the poet was to have an everlasting effect on the young painter. But as radical as his art seemed at the time, Manet was a reluctant revolutionary. His father was a magistrate, and Manet grew up haute bourgeoisie. After failing to qualify for law school, Manet was sent to study at the studio of Thomas Couture in the École des Beaux-Arts. Couture was a talented academic dauber whose historical painting, *Romans of the Decadence*, had been the hit of the Salon of 1847 and had actually been purchased by the government a year before completion.

Manet studied with Couture for six years, dutifully painting the models dressed as gods, but finally said to his fellow pupil Antonin Proust, "I don't know why I'm here. Everything we see around us is ridiculous. The light is false. The shadows are false. When I come into the studio, it seems to me that I am entering a tomb." Manet scoffed at Diderot's theory that in serious painting only historical clothing was worthy since contemporary clothing becomes unfashionable. Manet felt, "We must accept our times and paint what we see."

Charles Baudelaire (1821–1867) photographed by Nadar, 1862. France's greatest poet, he had a tremendous influence
on Manet and sometimes accompanied
him on sketching expeditions to the
Tuileries.

Edouard Manet (1832–1883), photographed by Nadar. The artist was more dandy than Bohemian.

Manet stubbornly insisted on posing the studio models in contemporary dress. When he had learned enough, he left Couture's atelier in 1856 and took his own studio in the Rue Lavoisier. He began to frequent cafés popular with other nonconformist painters and poets such as Gustave Courbet and Baudelaire.

For Baudelaire, the modern age was a time of dispersal and fragmentation, of individualism and lack of faith. Despite his modern vision, Baudelaire detested "progress" and sought escape in art, dandyism, and stimulants. One of Baudelaire's first essays was "Wine and Hashish compared as a means for the Multiplication of the Personality," published in 1851. In it he praised wine and disparaged hemp, but he soon became addicted to opium in the form of medicinal laudanum. "Paris taught him his vices, absinthe and opium, and the extravagant dandyism of his early manhood which involved him in debt the rest of his life," wrote

Tortoni's, the elegant café frequented by
the ever-social Manet. Later he would
move to the Café Guerbois and to the
Café de La Nouvelle-Athènes. A detail
from the lithograph by Eugène Guérard.

Manet's lithograph, *Le Café*, 1874, depicts the Café Guerbois, a famous meeting place for the impressionists. Cafés were gradually replacing the salon as the intellectuals' rendezvous.

Christopher Isherwood in the foreword to Baudelaire's *Intimate Journals*. But Paris also provided Baudelaire with poetic inspiration.

In 1857, Baudelaire was brought to trial and fined 300 francs after six of the poems in his book, *Les Fleurs du mal*, were alleged to be immoral. (Flaubert's *Madame Bovary* faced a similar fate the same year.) Baudelaire's book was a poetic study of evil and addiction by a man who saw the craving for sensation as the supreme characteristic of his age. The poems chronicle the journey of a sensual pilgrim whose mind is progressively dulled as he encounters lesbians, necrophiliacs, despair, and even dissatisfaction with death. Baudelaire was the first of a long series of artists to create beauty from the disorder of his life.

Like Baudelaire, Manet was a dandy and well-known in the cafés for his English-cut suits and top hat. But while hobnobbing with society and

Manet's engraving *The Absinthe
Drinker*, 1862.

intellectuals, he still had his eye on Paris street life. Sometime before 1857, Manet had noticed a shabby ragpicker called Collardet who used to beg for centimes on the steps of the Louvre. Manet thought the man's drunkenness possessed a curious nobility and asked him to pose for *The Absinthe Drinker.*

A few days before the painting was to be sent to the Salon of 1859, Manet invited his former teacher Couture to have a look at *The Absinthe Drinker.* The older artist stared at the painting and then at his former student. With growing alarm, he realized that the model was not an actor or fellow artist dressed as a ragpicker, but a real bum.

"An absinthe drinker!" he snorted. "And they paint abominations like that! My poor friend," Couture said shaking his head at Manet, "you are the absinthe drinker. It is you who have lost your moral faculty." When he left the studio with barely a good-by, both knew their already strained relationship was ending.

Actually, the salons of the late 1850s were filled with paintings of ragpickers, beggars, and drunks, while the beggar-philosopher had appeared in great Spanish and Flemish art since the seventeenth century. But what irked Couture and others was the insolent air of Manet's painting. Collardet was neither a jolly drinker nor a philosophical-looking old geezer. He was simply a bum — unrepentantly plastered on absinthe. Manet seemed to be ennobling decadence.

Again, the influence of Baudelaire is hard to ignore. In one of his poems, Baudelaire pays respect to the ragpickers who comb the great city, sifting through all the refuse of urban life, looking for anything worth a few centimes. Baudelaire ends the poem with what might be a self-portrait: "Il arrive hachant la tête et butant sur les Pavés comme les jeunes poètes qui passent toutes leurs journées à errer et à chercher des rimes." (He ends up bloodying his head and stumbling on the cobblestones like the young poets who spend all their days erring and searching for rhymes.)

As Antonin Proust recorded, a few days later, Baudelaire was in Manet's studio when word came that *The Absinthe Drinker* had been rejected by the Salon. Manet was upset and angrily accused Couture of influencing the jury, but Baudelaire replied, "La conclusion, c'est qu'il faut être soi-meme." (The conclusion is that you must be yourself.) Manet was heartened, however, at hearing a rumor that Delacroix (one of Baudelaire's heroes) had cast a vote in favor of the painting.

Baudelaire's *Les Paradis artificiels* (1860) had been mistaken as a celebration of decadence, when in fact, it was a condemnation of drugs and alcohol by a man who had discovered his own self-destruction too late. "I have come to loathe all stimulants because of the way they expand Time, and of the exaggeration with which they endow everything." Baudelaire warned modern man of the problems with drugs and stimulants, not so much for health reasons but for the highest philosophical premise. Drugs and alcohol disturbed man's natural fate in the universe and promised a world of debased but instant — hence, false — mysticism. "It is typical of modern man that he should accept this illusion, this stage-set paradise, as an adequate substitute for the real thing. Rather than devote himself to the long and difficult process of developing his spirituality, he wants instant results: to gain paradise at a stroke."

For all his knowledge about addictions, Baudelaire's own problems always seemed to get worse. While writing *Les Paradis artificiels*, he was taking laudanum, a tincture of opium, in the amount of 150 drops a day (seventy-five would have been fatal to a first-time user). Sensing the toll on his health and sanity, Baudelaire backed off the stimulants, but too late. "I have cultivated my hysteria with delight and terror. Now I suffer continually from vertigo, and today, 23rd of January 1862, I have received a singular warning, I have felt the wind of the wing of madness pass over me."

Baudelaire's early suspicion that he had been born under a dark star seemed to be fulfilling itself. He prayed to God for release from debt, disease, and spiritual failing. He even considered becoming a monk, but instead he went to Belgium. "One becomes a Belgian through having sinned," he wrote. "A Belgian is his own hell." He tried giving lectures on Delacroix and Gautier but frightened off his audience of matrons and school-children with a witty but off-color joke about virginity. In his Belgian exile, he took laudanum and drank absinthe to dull the vertigo and pain caused by syphilis. He was still optimistic about recovery, right up until he collapsed outside a church while walking with the artist Felicien Rops. Back in Paris, he was taken to a hospice run by nuns, but his slurred oaths of pain offended them and they uncharitably cast him out. He died at the age of forty-six on August 31, 1867.

Only sixty people attended the funeral in Montparnasse for the greatest poet France has ever known, but one of those men was Manet. And

Manet's portrait of Baudelaire in top
hat, 1862–1868. Etching, second plate,
second state.

17

An etching of Baudelaire by Manet,
1867.

after the poet's death, the journalist Victor Noir wrote, "In his last moments, his best friend was M. Manet; it was because the two natures understood each other so well."

Being a genius was not easy. After critics lambasted Manet's work in 1865, he had written to Baudelaire, "Insults are pouring down on me as thick as hail." Baudelaire tried to comfort Manet but worried about him: "Manet has strong talent, a talent which will resist. But he has a weak character. He seems disconsolate and dazed by the shock." John Canaday notes that Manet's struggle "marks the beginning of the modern artist as a man whose creative independence is subject to no check beyond his own conscience." Manet's *The Absinthe Drinker*, then, was a notorious debut for the modern age of painting, and the age of absinthe.

At the same time Manet was painting his absinthe drinker, a certain Dr. Motet was examining the first so-called *absinthistes* at Bicêtre, the leading psychiatric hospital in Paris; Motet eventually published his findings in an 1859 thesis called *Considérations générales sur l'alcoolisme et plus particulièrement des effets toxiques produits sur l'homme par la liqueur d'absinthe* (General considerations on alcoholism and more specifically of the toxic effects produced in man by the liquor absinthe).

Through observation of mental patients, Motet deduced that absinthe affected the heavy drinker in a manner distinct from other alcoholic drinks. Dr. Motet describes the case of one Jean-Baptiste S——, aged thirty-four, who entered his hospital on May 31, 1857:

"This man, of average height, in generally good health, had worked for three months as a sculptor on the exterior decoration of the Louvre. He was steady, sober, hard-working, when just fifteen days ago he left his circle of friends, and deserted work for the cabaret. He soon was drinking ten to twelve glasses of absinthe a day, then eau-de-vie, white wine, etc. Several days before his delirious attack, he drank again but without the ability to get drunk: he was like a beast. During the night of May 29–30, all of a sudden he jumped to the foot of his bed: he [imagined he] saw gendarmes coming to arrest him. He protested his innocence, then remained seated without saying anything until daylight.

"He was a little calmer near morning; he went out, drank absinthe, and returned in the evening in a completely besotted state. He was helped to bed, but no sooner was he in his bed than horrible

The bum in Manet's 1867 sketch, *Absinthe Drinker*, resembles Baudelaire, who died the same year. The poet's appetite for absinthe, hashish, and laudanum drove him to the edge of insanity, but he probably died of syphilis.

visions assailed him; he could not close his eyes for an instant without getting up, walking about the room, seeing enemies in the people who were trying to take care of him; as his state inspired alarm, he was taken the next day to an asylum."

Motet describes how the man's eyes remained bright, his skin hot, his head movements rapid. He did not seem to know exactly who he was, but he assured the medical attendants over and over that he was not guilty, that he had not killed anyone.

He remained wide awake all night. He never cried out but, speaking in a low voice, he described seeing "flames encircling his bed, grimacing faces detaching themselves from the walls. He was pursued by gendarmes ." (Motet, with curious precision, remarked, "Pas de visions d'animaux immondes." [No visions of filthy animals.])

He was given the standard treatment for the insane — hydrotherapy. He was put into a bath for five hours, and every half hour his head was doused with cold water. The baths continued for two days along with purges of Sedlitz water. Gradually, the nightmares diminished. A week later, he was calm enough to walk in the garden with the other patients. He seemed to comprehend that he had not been well but had no memory of what had transpired. He asked about his father and family. More baths and cold water dousings followed. Finally, when it was explained that he had been sick from excess of alcohol, he acknowledged the irregular life he had been leading, said he would change his habits, but still expressed a fear of being arrested and put in prison. Two weeks later he had "recovered" and was released.

Aside from telling us about the effects of absinthe, Motet's notes provide an interesting view of psychology in France at this time. Alcoholism, a problem which was almost unknown in that country before the nineteenth century, was so misunderstood that alcoholics were treated as insane and when "cured" and released, were told to drink only wine which was "healthy."

More detailed studies were conducted in 1864 by Dr. M. Marce at Bicêtre and by the illustrious Dr. Valentin Magnan of the asylum at Sainte-Anne in Paris. Of course, these early observations or experiments would not have been general knowledge to the public, but absinthe abuse was being noticed by social observers. Since psychology was still in its infancy and scientific researchers tended to focus on the clinical effects of absinthe, the only commentaries on the social effects of this drink at this time were provided by artists and novelists.

In 1860, a young Paris author and playwright, Henri Balesta, wrote *Absinthe et Absintheurs*. According to pharmacologist Dr. Ronald K. Siegel, this is probably the first known book to record the *socialization* of absinthe abuse. The year 1860, in fact, might be seen as a watershed for drug use throughout the world. In that same year, Britain enacted the Food and Drugs Act; British mycologist Mordecai Cooke published his classic work, *The Seven Sisters of Sleep*, warning against abuse of intoxicants; the United States legalized opium traffic with China; and coca and cocaine products started to appear throughout the Western world. Balesta was probably unaware of these events; yet as a young journalist about town, he sensed something happening in Paris's appetite for absinthe.

Balesta's ninety-four page book was divided into seven chapters describing various case studies of absinthe drinking in Parisian society, ending with Balesta's own anti-absinthe appeal. In one chapter, Balesta details the plight of one Monsieur Aubin, a widowed cabinet maker from the Faubourg Sainte-Antoine, who out of loneliness, frequents the cafés and inadvertently makes an absinthe addict out of his six-year-old daughter. "He loved his daughter too much to leave her alone or to leave her with hired help, but he did not love her enough to give up his new pleasures."

One day, the absinthe-loving Monsieur Aubin finds a way to bring the quiet, pale child out of her sorrow for her dead mother. "He had a diabolical idea. Calling the little one to him, he offered her a glass of absinthe, saying: 'Come on sweetheart, drink, that will give you strength and color in your cheeks.'"

Within a short time, the child is addicted to the drink. "She was the first one to demand her share if they forgot to give it to her, and at times she drank up to two glasses of absinthe in a single evening. But soon a reaction set in, and it was a terrible one. The most alarming symptoms appeared: anxieties, a heaviness in the region of the chest, febrile movements, paralysis of the stomach."

Maddened with terror, Aubin runs for a doctor who guesses the terrible truth in a single examination of the young patient. "He took the father aside, questioned him closely and drew out a complete confession. 'Now listen,' he said to him, 'you have wasted your daughter by overstimulating her; in a month she will have lived out her life and it is you that have killed her, you, her father

Honoré Daumier's 1863 caricature of two absinthe drinkers is captioned "Le premier verre, le sixième verre" (The first glass and the sixth glass). Manet admired Daumier greatly.

who ought to have protected her. I pray that you will never regret it.'"

But it is too late. As the doctor had predicted, the child died three weeks later. The day after the funeral, Aubin was found hanged in his garret. "Condemned by remorse, he had atoned for his crime."

Balesta was even better at describing the drinking habits of café society in Paris: "In the morning, at lunchtime, the habitués invaded the bistro. The professors of absinthe were already at their station, yes, the teachers of absinthe, for it is a science, or rather an art to drink absinthe properly, and certainly to drink it in quantity. They put themselves on the trail of the novice drinkers, teaching them to raise their elbow high and frequently, to water their absinthe artistically, and when, after the tenth little glass, the pupil rolled under the table, the master went on to another, always drinking, always holding forth, always steady and unshakeable at his post."

In the end Balesta's typical absinthe drinker ends up a total addict: "He drinks it in the morning, he drinks it at noon, he drinks it in the evening, he drinks it at night, he drinks it all the time. He drinks it when he is happy to celebrate his happiness. He drinks it when he is sad to kill his sadness. But, alas, nothing vibrates any more in him, everything is empty, everything is dead, only remorse, that last wreckage of his sinking, still survives."

At the time Balesta was writing (and for the next decade), absinthe was a relatively expensive drink compared to wine. But when absinthe producers brought out cheaper (and more dangerous) concoctions, the price dropped and the average man could afford it. For example, in 1873 a glass of absinthe cost only fifteen centimes while a kilo of bread was fifty centimes and a bottle of good Bordeaux might be a whole franc. Balesta's observations on class distinctions among absinthe drinkers also predict the way fin de siècle socialist politicians would denounce absinthe as a poisoner of the working class:

"And do not think that absinthomania is the vice peculiar to the rich and idle of your society.

The man of the people, the workman, has not been spared its ravages. He too has given himself up, bound hand and foot, to the demons who tempt him. And yet, how much disaster do the vices of the poor bring in their train! The rich, the idle, the useless must find ways to kill time, their deadliest enemy; if he occasionally kills himself, what does it matter? He dies alone, he is not linked to anyone, it only concerns himself.

"But the poor man, he drags five, ten lives with him, and his father, and his mother, both ailing who nourished him as a child so that he could care for them in their old age, and his wife and children. . . . He borrows on tomorrow's wages. . . . He drinks to drown his sorrows, he drinks to forget, and, that night, when he staggers back to his slum, the children ask for bread, his wife reproaches him for his idleness. Fury grips him, an anger all the stronger because he is at fault and he knows it. He raises his hand against the poor wife who has joined her misery to his, he strikes her as a reward for ten years of devotion."

Little by little, Balesta brings the sad tale to a close, and the last shred of morality is blown away: "His daughter? He encounters her one night, coming out of a cabaret, dressed in silk and dragging her shameful luxury along the pavement of the boulevard."

Balesta was an impressionable young man when he wrote *Absinthe et Absintheurs*. Over the next half-century, he watched absinthe consumption increase fiftyfold in France. Not much is known about Balesta's life, except that he wrote a book in 1883 about two famous crimes and published plays and short stories about Parisian life before disappearing into obscurity. But in 1906, Balesta wrote a curious play entitled *The Serum* in which he envisioned the creation of the ideal elixir that might have corrected the problems of absinthism. Ronald K. Siegel described the irony of this in a recent article: "While the absinthe of 1860 made users old and mad, Balesta's fictitious drug of 1906 had the magical ability to change the old and mad into the young and passionate. But, like all such artificial intoxicants, even the 'ideal' serum led to abuse and social dysfunction."

Opposite: Emile Benasset's lithograph, *L'Absinthe*, 1862, depicts absinthe flowing from a death's head fountain.

Paul Marie Verlaine in seemingly fine
form, between absinthe binges.

Chapter 3

Absinthe and the Poets: Verlaine, Rimbaud, Wilde, and Dowson

Of all the French poets, Paul Marie Verlaine was most responsible for building a Bohemian cult around absinthe. Verlaine's alcoholic tendency appeared when he was in his teens, and soon he developed a nearly unquenchable thirst for the drink. Absinthe gave him a sense of exaltation that he injected into his poetry, but it also made him violent and unpredictable.

The death of his cousin Elisa Moncomble in February 1867 had a profound effect on Verlaine. Elisa had helped finance the publication of his *Poèmes saturniens* and, though married, she had always been an object of Verlaine's love. Her death sent him reeling. "Yes, in the three days after the burial of my dear cousin, I couldn't keep myself together except by drinking beer after beer," wrote Verlaine to a friend. "I became a drunk . . . so much so that returning to Paris where the beer is awful, it was upon absinthe that I threw myself, absinthe day and night."

While heavy drinking and explosive tempers ran in his father's family, his mother's clan was pious and orderly — a trait which revealed itself in an odd fashion: having suffered three miscarriages before Paul's birth in 1844, Madame Verlaine preserved the fetuses in jars. Young Verlaine's sexual impulses drew him first to prostitutes, then to men, which led to guilt and drinking. In 1869, he violently attacked his mother and finally smashed her fetus-bearing jars. That same year, he met and married Mathilde Mauté, half-sister of Charles de Sivry. No doubt the poet was seeking in the seventeen-year-old girl some illusion of grace and purity, but as Voltaire wrote in *Zadig*, "The first month of marriage is the honeymoon, and the second is the absinthe-moon."

Everything changed in September 1871, when Arthur Rimbaud arrived in Paris. Rimbaud was a sixteen-year-old aspiring poet without a penny to his name but a satchelful of wonderful poems. He had read books on the occult and was mesmerized by Baudelaire's vision of life as a simultaneous experience of insistent flesh and searching spirit. "It is through dreaming that man communicates with the dark dream by which he is surrounded," Rimbaud announced.

By November, Verlaine and Rimbaud were inseparable, much to Mathilde's distress.

Although Baudelaire later denounced the merits of dreams inspired by intoxication, the young Rimbaud mistakenly imagined that Baudelaire had earned freedom from moral inhibition through his use of addictive substances. Rimbaud believed that the poet had to deprive and degrade

Since he has cultivated his soul — richer to begin with than any other! He arrives at the unknown: and even if, half-crazed, in the end, he loses the understanding of his visions, he has seen them!"

In his early days in Paris, Rimbaud lived in the streets scavenging like a bum. What little money he had was spent drinking in the cafés. In a June 1872 letter to Ernest Delahaye, he wrote: "There is a drinking place I prefer: long live L'Académie d'Absomphe, in spite of the ill-temper of the waiters! It is the most delicate and trembling of all vestments, this drunkenness by virtue of the sagebrush of the glaciers, *absomphe*!" (L'Académie d'Absinthe was a café formerly at 176 Rue Saint-Jacques; "absomphe" was Rimbaud's comic spelling of absinthe.)

Only by drinking absinthe in excess, could the poet fuse the Apollonian and Dionysian spheres. In 1872, Rimbaud wrote a ballad about drinking, "Comédie de la Soif" (Comedy of thirst):

Come, the Wines go to the beaches,
And the waves by the millions!
See the wild Bitter
Rolling from the top of the mountains!
Let us, wise pilgrims, reach
The Absinthe with the green pillars . . .

Arthur Rimbaud was photographed by Carjat shortly after his arrival in Paris in 1871. Rimbaud wounded Carjat one night with a sword cane.

himself, to become morbid compost from which art would spring like enchanted mushrooms. While Baudelaire maintained a sense of sin, Rimbaud felt the real poet would sacrifice all, from honor to sanity, to become a visionary.

In an 1872 letter to Paul Démeny, Rimbaud observed: "The poet makes himself a seer through a long, prodigious and rational disordering of all the senses. Every form of love, of suffering, of madness; he searches himself, he consumes all the poisons in him, keeping only their quintessences. Ineffable torture in which he will need all his faith and superhuman strength, the great criminal, the great sickman, the utterly damned, and the supreme Savant! For he arrives at the Unknown!

By most accounts, Verlaine and Rimbaud were besotted on a nearly full-time basis. For Rimbaud, drinking was not a pleasure but a necessary form of flagellation to make the nerves sing like harp wires. Verlaine had a different temperament. When absinthe percolated through his system, he behaved with loathsome brutality, taking out a deep-seated anger on his passive wife Mathilde. He beat her, set fire to her hair and clothes, and even slashed her with a knife. Rimbaud urged Verlaine on, persuading him that there was nothing more ridiculous in this world than a "good family man" — a true seeker would not cater to domesticity.

Frightened by her husband's behavior, Mathilde showed a cache of Verlaine's letters from the surly Rimbaud to Dr. Antoine Cros, brother of the poet-inventor Charles Cros (who himself wrote a poem about absinthe). Dr. Cros read them and thought Verlaine and Rimbaud were unbalanced by their absinthe abuse. Mathilde's fears increased when Antoine Cros told her what hap-

André Gill spoofed the military appetite
for absinthe in *L'Éclipse*, June 21, 1874.
Rimbaud, who admired Gill's work,
looked him up on his arrival in Paris in
1871, and mooched a few nights on his
sofa. Gill also helped him financially.

Verlaine and Rimbaud traveled to London in September 1872 but soon quarreled and separated. Drawing by Félix Regamey.

pened a few weeks earlier during an absinthe binge:

"We were all three at the Café du Rat Mort, Verlaine, Rimbaud, and I, when Rimbaud said to us: 'Put your hands on the table, I want to show you an experiment.' We thought it was a joke, and put out our hands; he pulled an open clasp-knife from his pocket and cut Verlaine's wrists quite deeply. I had time to take my hands away and I wasn't hurt. Verlaine left with his sinister companion and received two other stab-wounds in his thigh."

Rimbaud was a pest. He kept lice in his hair to throw on priests, and at poetry readings he perversely shouted "Merde!" as punctuation to each line that bored him. He once attacked the photographer Carjat with a sword cane (but did little damage). As he grew tired of Verlaine's senti-

mentalism, Rimbaud played similar tricks on the older poet. While Verlaine seemed to thrive on this abuse, the rest of the literary set were naturally offended by Rimbaud's scatological insolence. Verlaine's café companions liked to consider themselves "Bohemians" but believed in boundaries of conduct.

On September 7, 1872, Verlaine and Rimbaud went to London where they consorted with the artists and political exiles from the Paris Commune of 1870. But within days, Verlaine was sending Edmond Lepelletier impressions of the stifling Victorian capital whose restaurants and coffee houses were unlicensed to sell liquor. "'We don't have spirits,' replied a maid to whom I put this insidious question: 'One absinthe, if you please, mademoiselle.'"

A year later, Rimbaud broke off the rela-

(oh la la !... C'est plus des javanais qu'il me faut !.....

[sur le 70e parallèle]

Ernest Delahaye's fanciful drawing of Rimbaud drinking absinthe with a polar bear refers to the 1877 trip the poet made to Sweden where he joined a traveling circus, Cirque Loisset.

tionship. In despair, Verlaine fled to Brussels where he wrote Rimbaud that he would commit suicide. In Brussels on July 8, Rimbaud found Verlaine in a state of great intoxication and excitement. Rimbaud was suddenly disgusted by the pleading, drunken poet and spent two days trying to convince Verlaine they must separate voluntarily. Verlaine drank himself into a stupor, but the next morning he got up early and returned at noon with a newly purchased revolver. Drunk again, Verlaine told Rimbaud he intended to "shoot everybody." Rimbaud tried to say good-by, but the furious Verlaine locked the door and seated himself in a chair, blocking his exit. "Now try to go," he said, "and you'll see what will happen!" He whipped out the pistol and fired three times.

The first bullet struck Rimbaud in the wrist, but the others went wide. As Rimbaud bled on the floor, Verlaine realized what he had done, wept violently, and fled down the hall of the hotel to his mother's room. Madame Verlaine and Rimbaud managed to control Verlaine, and Rimbaud patched himself up. But as Rimbaud was leaving to catch a train for Paris, Verlaine took the pistol again and threatened to kill him. This time, Rimbaud called a policeman, and Verlaine was arrested. During the police investigation, their sodomitical relations were revealed, and Verlaine was sentenced to five years in prison.

For Rimbaud, the days of absinthe and Verlaine were over. He suffered a major character crisis and wrote his final salute to visionary poetry, *Une Saison en enfer* (A Season in Hell). He felt that his experiences had been madness, folly, destructive magic. He burned his manuscripts and looked for a way to start over, to live anew. In her remark-

The Absinthe Drinkers by Jean-François Raffaëlli, a friend of Degas.

able biography of Rimbaud, Enid Starkie contends Rimbaud believed that he had acquired supernatural powers; that, like Faust, he had become the equal of God; and that eventually his sins of pride and arrogance had been as great and as deserving of condemnation. Rimbaud had once believed poetry to be magic, a tool to penetrate the unknown. When he relinquished poetry, he gave up the last real happiness in his life.

In January of 1875, Verlaine was released from prison, his sentence reduced for good conduct. His wife despised him, his literary colleagues shunned him, and Verlaine's thoughts turned to Rimbaud once more. Verlaine tracked Rimbaud to Stuttgart where he was studying German and his early interest, the occult. While in prison, Verlaine had experienced a religious awakening and now wrote a letter to Rimbaud begging him to embrace Catholicism.

Rimbaud consented to a visit from Verlaine but wrote blasphemously about the reunion: "The other day Verlaine arrived in Stuttgart, with a

Albert Maignan's *The Green Muse,*
1895, shows a poet succumbing to the
charms of the Green Fairy. Note the
glass on his desk and the broken bottle.

Rimbaud in Harar, one of the last photographs of him alive. He put aside poetry for a life of action in Africa, transforming himself into a hard-bitten gunrunner and colonial explorer.

rosary in his paws, but three hours later he denied God, and made the ninety-six wounds of our Blessed Lord bleed again." They went from bar to bar until Verlaine's old violence surfaced again. Down by the river at night, Verlaine tried to kiss Rimbaud and was pushed away. Angered, Verlaine attacked him. Rimbaud, no longer a skinny adolescent but a grown man, knocked Verlaine unconscious. The next morning some peasants found Verlaine lying in the dirt and took him into town. Weeping and calling Rimbaud a messenger from Satan, Verlaine returned to Paris and wrote to Rimbaud in an evangelical tone. "The Church has fashioned modern civilization, science, and literature. She also made France what she is, and France is now dying because she has broken with her."

Rimbaud never replied. He went to Holland in 1876, enlisted in the Dutch army, and sailed for Java, where he deserted at the first opportunity to become a seaman. In Egypt he carved his name in a pillar at Luxor and in Cyprus he worked as a foreman on a construction crew. Rimbaud became a man Joseph Conrad might have written about: a man of action, a tough trader in Somalia and Abyssinia, going into regions no other white man had ever been. He was important to the colonial expansion in these countries and was implicated in slave traffic and the illicit gun trade. He dealt in coffee and animal hides. He lead a roving, hard-bitten existence far from poetic fancy.

In 1890, suffering from an abscessed leg, he returned to France by ship and was met at

Verlaine in an absinthe stupor in the Café Procope. Beside the inkwell stands a glass of his "humble ephemeral absinthe."

Marseilles by his mother and sister. The leg was amputated, but a mysterious disease, perhaps carcinoma or a complication of syphilis, spread and paralyzed him. After a few cruel months, he made a deathbed conversion to Catholicism.

As he lay failing in his bed, Rimbaud described to his sister the brilliant amethyst-tiered visions he was seeing. He prayed constantly, and a priest came to take his confession. He died on November 9, 1891, three weeks before his thirty-seventh birthday. No men of letters, not even Verlaine, attended his funeral. Most people thought he had died years before.

While in prison Verlaine had vowed never to drink absinthe again and for the next few years he took nothing but beer and worked steadily on his poetry. But soon absinthe made its way back into his life. In a letter to Stéphane Mallarmé he apologized: "In haste, on my travels, I happen to be in a tavern. . . . Still sugared, confused. Very worried. Excuse all horrors." The sugared absinthe was once more before him at the table.

In the 1890s, Verlaine became the vagabond king of the Latin Quarter. And like a royal presence, he had a court jester, Bibi-la-Purée (a.k.a. André Salis), a bootblack and street scavenger who resembled a grotesque from a Breughel painting. There was something touching about their relationship, as Louis Roseyre recorded in *Au temps du quartier:*

"Bibi-la-Purée came first, clearing a way through the crowd, so that the reeling poet . . .

33

Under the Spell, by Guillaume, 1908.

could find a seat. Verlaine followed, painfully, dragging his leg, and leaning on a stout stick. . . . He collapsed onto a chair. . . . Suddenly my heart, the heart of a boy of eighteen, bled with grief and fear at the sight of this old man, whining and infirm, demanding another absinthe. I knew the legend; but really Verlaine, this man who was trembling all over, this man with a dirty beard, his face half-hidden by a filthy muffler, . . . Verlaine collapsing on Bibi-la-Purée, with that horrible, grinning face, and mouth slit to the ears, Bibi smelling of rat, old rotting rat! . . . I have never been able to forget that sinister and pitiful vision."

Verlaine held court in the Café François Ier in the Boulevard Saint-Michel or sometimes in La Procope. The prostitutes and students would point Verlaine out like some tourist attraction, as he sat smoking a cheap cigar, his "humble, ephemeral absinthe" always before him. He would emerge from a stupor to recite poetry or to suggest to the

young poets around him that they prove their admiration with a five franc piece. At the Café Vachette he would introduce the prostitutes to literature, advising them to read Descartes.

In an early poem, Verlaine associated himself with Don Quixote, the champion of illusions whom he called, "old paladin, grand bohème." As Jerrold Seigel noted, for Verlaine, "The lonely knight's death was a martyrdom, his life a poem; he beckoned poets to assault the heights of fantasy and praised poetry's victory over inept reason. Here Bohemia stood for the liberation of dream life and the abolition of boundaries, especially that between imagination and reality."

Intoxication by absinthe was a shortcut to dream life, but even Verlaine was certainly not unaware of the negative aspects of absinthe on his health. He once described his friend, the emaciated composer Cabaner, whose face consisted of little more than a diaphanous beard and a pair of

34

Le Boulevard, La Nuit, by Jean Béraud
evokes the elegance of Paris in the Belle
Époque.

dreamy eyes, as looking like "Jesus Christ after three years of absinthe." Unlike many poets of his generation, Verlaine never used hashish, opium, ether, or morphine, which were in fashion and easy to come by. Verlaine actually expressed a horror of these "poisons." With rare exceptions, he never drank anything but absinthe, beer, or rum-and-water. Although many journalists maliciously exaggerated his drinking, he was more or less drunk every day. "I get drunk to keep up my reputation," Verlaine assured the novelist Jules Renard. "And I am a slave to my reputation."

Verlaine would tell anyone who bought him a drink about his love for the Green Fairy. He once wrote:

> For me, my glory is but an
> "humble ephemeral absinthe"
> drunk on the sly, with fear of treason
> and if I drink it no longer,
>   it is for a good reason.

While Verlaine taught school to earn money, he "adopted" and later seduced one of his students, Lucien Létinois, not for his intellect but because he reminded Verlaine of Rimbaud. They were together for six years, Verlaine alternating between father-figure and dominating satyr. While he gained a certain reputation as a mystic Catholic poet, some of the critics spotted a spiritual sleight of hand in Verlaine's book *Sagesse*; the confessional poems seemed to have a tone of reminiscence rather than repentance for past sins.

Verlaine never got over Rimbaud. In 1884, Verlaine published a book, *Les Poètes maudits*, which greatly enhanced Rimbaud's literary reputation. But by 1885, Verlaine had become destitute, and the religious inspiration faded from the poems. The journalist Gabriel de Lautrec sometimes took Verlaine to dinner and, if he was on good behavior, out for a drink. "After many peregrinations, we reached the Place Maubert.

Oscar Wilde at his most seductive, while touring America in 1882. He once said, "Absinthe has a wonderful color, green. A glass of absinthe is as poetical as anything in the world. What difference is there between a glass of absinthe and a sunset?"

There was a bar where they sold absinthe at four sous a glass. I never dared ask what these absinthes were made of. . . . But Verlaine was content."

During his last years, Verlaine was in and out of hospitals suffering from his absinthe habit and any number of diseases including cirrhosis of the liver, pneumonia, rheumatism, gonorrhea, and syphilis. In a letter sent from the hospital to his friend and publisher Vanier, Verlaine wrote: "Received back here like the prodigal son. Mild reproaches, that's all. And arrived in very good shape in spite of all the absinthe." The nurses would overlook the small bottles of absinthe his friends tucked under his pillow; they knew small amounts made little difference now. Yet before his death in 1896, even Verlaine denounced absinthe as "the source of folly and crime, of idiocy and shame which governments should tax heavily if they don't abolish it."

Verlaine and Oscar Wilde had two things in common: both drank absinthe with a passion and both were jailed for their homosexuality. But when they met in Paris at the Café Vachette in 1883, Wilde was at the height of his dandyism, the hit of the London stage, and the darling of the English drawing room. Verlaine was in bad shape, depressed over the death of his lover Lucien Létinois, and dressed in a seedy fashion. Wilde was put off by the poet's shabby appearance but recognized his genius. It probably never occurred to Wilde that one day he would fall further in the world than Verlaine.

Upon his return to Paris in 1891, Wilde took the literary salons by storm. His guide was a young journalist of the day, Marcel Schwob, who introduced him to everyone important. Léon Daudet received Wilde at his house in Paris and wrote that "his voice was at once pallid and fat, words came tumbling out of his frightful slack mouth and when he would finish he would roar with laughter like a fat, satisfied, gossipy woman." Edmond de Goncourt described him as "an individual of doubtful sex who talks like a third rate actor."

Even Schwob, who respected Wilde's writing and dedicated a book to him, described him without rapture: "A big man, with a large pasty face, red cheeks, an ironic eye, bad and protrusive teeth, a vicious childlike mouth with lips soft with milk ready to suck more. While he ate — and he ate little — he never stopped smoking opium-tainted Egyptian cigarettes. A terrible absinthe-drinker, through which he gets his visions."

Oscar Wilde and his lover, "Bosie," Lord Alfred Douglas, in Oxford, 1893. Douglas's father exposed their affair, leading to Wilde's imprisonment and ruin. In later years, Douglas renounced homosexuality, married, and tried to hide the truth about his relationship with Wilde.

One day, Wilde, the man who said "Little boys should be obscene and not heard," found himself at the center of scandal. He was charged with practicing "indecent acts" with Lord Alfred Douglas, son of the marquess of Queensberry. Wilde boldly tried to sue Queensberry for libel, but the marquess, a sportsman who had written the rules for English boxing, was a vengeful man who would not be crossed. Wilde was convicted of sodomy, partially on the decadent character of his writings such as the *The Picture of Dorian Gray*, and was sentenced harshly to two years in Reading Gaol.

Upon his release in 1897, Wilde was refused a retreat with English Jesuits and finally fled the ostracism of London for France. In Dieppe he was snubbed by the English artists Aubrey Beardsley and Walter Sickert. In Paris, former friends André Gide and Stuart Merrill, both homosexuals, ignored him while the painter James A. McNeill Whistler was embarrassed to run into him at a restaurant. Wilde resorted to a furtive existence, assuming the name Sebastian Melmoth, taken from his uncle Reverend Charles Maturin's novel *Melmoth the Wanderer*, the story of a man who bargains with Satan, exchanging his soul for life and is doomed to wander for a hundred years as a vampire. Wilde once told Max de Morès, "I am a vagabond. The century will have had two vagabonds, Paul Verlaine and me."

And while he wandered, Wilde drank absinthe, once describing to a friend the effect it had on him: "After the first glass you see things as you wish they were. After the second, you see things as they are not. Finally you see things as they really are, and that is the most horrible thing in the world."

In 1897, Wilde developed a crush on the thirty-year-old poet Ernest Christopher Dowson who was over to spend the winter away from London; but Dowson was not interested and urged Wilde to try women again. After a visit to a whore in Dieppe, Wilde told Dowson, "It was like chewing

The poet, Ernest Dowson, said, "Absinthe makes the tart grow fonder."

ABSINTHIA TAETRA

By Ernest Dowson

Green changed to white, emerald to opal; nothing was changed.

The man let the water trickle gently into his glass, and as the green clouded, a mist fell from his mind.

Then he drank opaline.

Memories and terrors beset him. The past tore after him like a panther and through the blackness of the present he saw the luminous tiger eyes of the things to be.

But he drank opaline.

And that obscure night of the soul, and the valley of humiliation, through which he stumbled, were forgotten. He saw blue vistas of undiscovered countries, high prospects and a quiet, caressing sea. The past shed its perfume over him, to-day held his hand as if it were a little child, and to-morrow shone like a white star: nothing was changed.

He drank opaline.

The man had known the obscure night of the soul, and lay even now in the valley of humiliation; and the tiger menace of the things to be was red in the skies. But for a little while he had forgotten.

Green changed to white, emerald to opal: nothing was changed.

cold mutton." Then as an afterthought he added, "But tell it in England, where it will entirely restore my reputation."

Dowson borrowed money from Wilde and did not repay him for months, but when someone criticized Dowson, saying, "It's a pity he drinks so much absinthe," Wilde just shrugged his shoulders and replied, "If he didn't drink, he would be somebody else. Personality must be accepted for what it is. You mustn't mind that a poet is a drunk, rather that drunks are not always poets."

Dowson had trouble with absinthe and wrote the story-poem "Absinthia Taetra" after the winter of 1897 when, as Mark Longaker wrote, "He drank to excess not because he liked the squalid and the evil but, like many another, because he was ill in body and soul." The poem is a sort of "Confessions of an English Absinthe Drinker" and in light of Dowson's absinthe habits, cannot be dismissed as a rhetorical exercise.

A contemporary of Dowson quoted the poet as saying: "Whiskey and beer are for fools; absinthe for poets; absinthe has the power of the magicians; it can wipe out or renew the past, and annul or foretell the future."

In a less enthusiastic letter, he wrote, "On the whole it is a mistake to get binged on the verdant fluid. As a steady drink it is inferior to the homely Scotch . . . awoke this morning with jingling nerves and a pestilential mouth on. . . . I understand absinthe makes the tart grow fonder. It is extremely detrimental to the complexion. . . . I never presented a more deboshed [*sic*] appearance than I do this morning."

Dowson's death on February 23, 1900 deeply affected Wilde who wrote to his publisher, Leonard Smithers: "Poor wounded wonderful fellow that he was: a tragic reproduction of all tragic poetry, like a symbol, or a scene. I hope bay-leaves will be laid on his tomb, and rue, and myrtle too, for he knew what love is."

Wilde's epic poem about prison, *The Ballad of Reading Gaol*, was a great success, but it was his swansong to literature. He stopped writing, spending his days reading Balzac in his shabby room at the Hotel d'Alsace or making forays to cafés for absinthes. Occasionally, he would snare a stray boy. His closest friend was his literary executor, Robert Ross, who years before had been the first to initiate Wilde to homosexual practices. Wilde became a restless soul moving from one café to another.

The Absinthe Drinker, circa 1910, by
Sir William Orpen, an Irish artist.

The Glass of Absinthe, 1905, by Albert
Rutherston, an English painter.

Wilde's attitude towards absinthe, as Richard
Ellmann noted in his recent biography, varied
depending upon whom he was speaking to and
when. "It has no message for me," he told the art
connoisseur Bernard Berenson. But to Arthur
Machen he said, "I never could quite accustom
myself to absinthe, but it suits my style so well."
Yet later he told someone in Dieppe, "Absinthe
has a wonderful color, green. A glass of absinthe is
as poetical as anything in the world. What difference is there between a glass of absinthe and a
sunset?"

As Wilde slid into poverty, he was forced to
beg from friends and was further snubbed by the
English community. "I was a problem for which
there was no solution," Wilde once said. Like
many of the artists of his time, Wilde also had a
problem for which medical science had no solution: syphilis. And in the fall of 1900, this malady
developed into a serious mastoidal infection.

Two weeks after an operation on his ear, he was
haggard and thin but witty as ever, announcing to

"WHO SIT AT THE LITTLE MARBLE TABLES, DRINK ABSINTHE, AND ARE INVARIABLY DECORATED." *Harper's Magazine, April 1889*

Absinthe drinkers in *Harper's* Magazine, April 1889.

Claire de Pratz, "My wallpaper and I are fighting a duel to the death. One of us has to go." But alarmed by his drinking, Robert Ross said, "You'll kill yourself Oscar. You know the doctor said absinthe was poison for you." Wilde sadly replied, "And what have I to live for, Robbie?"

The next day Wilde had a cold and continuing pain in his ear but insisted on a carriage ride through the Bois du Boulogne and on drinking absinthe in a café. An abscess developed in the ear, possibly a result of tertiary syphilis. Despite a specialist's efforts, Wilde developed meningitis and became delirious. The prescibed morphine did not help, only opium and chloral gave him relief, and he drank champagne rather than absinthe. One day, Wilde awakened and told Ross and a friend, Reggie Turner, "I dreamt I was supping with the dead." Turner replied, "My dear Oscar, you were probably the life and soul of the party."

Three weeks earlier, Wilde, who was raised as an Anglican, had told a journalist, "Much of my moral obliquity is due to the fact that my father

would not allow me to become a Catholic. The artistic side of the Church and the fragrance of its teaching would have cured my degeneracies. I intend to be received before long." Now the anxious Ross, a Catholic himself, summoned a priest. Wilde was no longer able to speak, but when asked if he wished to be received by the church, he held up his hand. The priest gave Wilde conditional baptism, and absolved and anointed him. He died on November 30 and was buried on December 3 at the cemetery in Bagneux; in 1909 his body was moved to Paris's Père-Lachaise Cemetery. On the tomb sculpted by Sir Jacob Epstein are engraved these words from *Reading Gaol*:

> And alien tears will fill for him
> Pity's long-broken urn,
> For his mourners will be outcast men,
> And outcasts always mourn.

41

Edgar Degas's famous *L'Absinthe*, 1876.
The models were Degas's friends, actress
Ellen Andrée and artist Marcellin Desboutin. In 1893 the picture roused
intense Francophobia in London.

Chapter 4

Degas Takes Absinthe to London

"hat a slut!" said George Moore, adding priggishly, "The tale is not a pleasant one, but is a lesson."

The "tale" was told by Edgar Degas's famous *L'Absinthe*, painted in 1876, a picture which set off one of the silliest rumpuses in the London art world in 1893. The "slut" was actress Ellen Andrée, portrayed in a Paris café called La Nouvelle-Athènes. The "lesson," one supposes, was not to drink too much absinthe. George Moore, an Irish man of letters, had spent his youth in Paris with the crowd at the Nouvelle-Athènes and had been painted three times by Manet. Though a full initiate to Bohemia, Moore had to backpedal in order to defend Degas in his English newspaper article. His declaration that the picture was a "lesson" was a rather typical remark of the Victorian age.

Ironically, in previous years Degas had enjoyed the lion's share of the meager appreciation London dealt the French impressionists, and English critics such as Frederick Wedmore called Degas in 1883 "the master of the Impressionist School, the man of genius, the inspirer of the whole party." Degas had many friends in London in the 1870s, among them the painters James Tissot, James A. McNeill Whistler, and Alphonse Legros. More of

his pictures were shown in London than those of his colleagues and by 1876 the English collector Captain Henry Hill of Brighton had formed the largest collection of Degas's work in all of Europe, including *L'Absinthe*.

In Paris, Degas was a member of Manet's circle, first at the Café de Bade, then at the Café Guerbois, and later at the illustrious Nouvelle-Athènes. The intellectual exchange in these cafés exerted an enormous influence on the arts of the time. Claude Monet never had the feeling of having wasted his time in the café and said, "You always left better steeled, your willpower firmer still, your thoughts clearer, more distinct." Manet and Degas shared ideas, and a friendly rivalry sprang up between them. It was with some pleasure that Degas would later claim to have beaten Manet to certain subject matter from real life such as horse-racing scenes.

Instead of painting an absinthe-drinking bum like Manet's Collardet, Degas painted his café companions, the actress Ellen Andrée and the engraver Marcellin Desboutin. A well-known character in Bohemian circles, Desboutin initiated the migration from the Café Guerbois to the Nouvelles-Athènes on the Place Pigalle. Desboutin was a curious figure who, like Manet and Degas, was from a wealthy middle class family and had

Edgar Hilaire Degas as a young man.

given up the study of law for art, joining Courbet's studio as a student. For years he had lived in an immense villa near Florence, the Ombrellino, where he entertained lavishly and wrote plays until he ran out of money. Returning to Paris, Desboutin saw his drama, *Maurice de Saxe*, play at the Comédie-Française for a few successful days in 1870, but it was interrupted by war. He made a living as a painter and etcher, and though wretched in appearance, he was an ardent monarchist with courtly manners.

Comparing Degas's absinthe picture to Manet's, painted seventeen years earlier, one sees readily the changes that have occurred in pictorial sensibilities. Manet placed his figure in a traditional space reminiscent of Velázquez, while Degas's composition has a calculated offhandedness, like a snapshot. Degas, like Lautrec, actually did rely on photographs to paint. The cropped aspect of the picture points clearly to photographic influence and to the radical compositions of Japanese prints that were becoming popular in Paris.

Though Degas eschewed literary sources, his café scene recalls the words of Baudelaire: "Though I have sung the mad pleasures of wine and opium, I thirst only for a liquor unknown on earth which the pharmaceutics of heaven itself could not afford me; a liquor that contains neither vitality nor death, neither excitation nor extinction. To know nothing, to will nothing, to sleep and still to sleep, this today is my only wish. A base and loathsome wish, but sincere."

Degas's picture was less a portrait of friends than a picture of a time and a place: it was l'heure verte in any Montmartre café. In his excellent book on Paris, Ian Littlewood quotes turn-of-the-century writer H.P. Hugh on this quarter of Paris:

"The sickly odour of absinthe lies heavily in the air. The 'absinthe' hour of the Boulevards begins vaguely at half-past-five, and it ends just as vaguely at half-past-seven; but on the hill it never ends. Not that it is a home of the drunkard in any way; but the deadly opal drink lasts longer than anything else, and it is the aim of Montmartre to stop as long as possible on the *terrasse* of a café and watch the world go by. To spend an hour in a really typical haunt of the Bohemians is a liberal education. There is none of the reckless gaiety of the Latin quarter, but at the same time there is a grim delight in chaffing at death and bankruptcy."

This was the Montmartre of Zola's novel, *Nana*: that superb courtesan Nana who, when not walking the streets, would sit in her room on the

Manet's unfinished oil portrait, *George Moore (Au Café)*. The Irish man of letters who frequented La Nouvelle-Athènes, called Ellen Andrée a "slut" during the hullaballoo over Degas's picture.

Left: Self-portrait by Degas's friend, Marcellin Desboutin.

Sarah Bernhardt was furious when her image appeared in an Absinthe Terminus poster without permission. She won a lawsuit and had the posters torn down.

Rue de la Rochefoucauld, drinking absinthe and gossiping with her lesbian friend Satin. It was in this world that absinthe gained its reputation as an aphrodisiac.

"I did not go to either Oxford or Cambridge, but I went to the Nouvelle-Athènes," wrote George Moore. "I can hear the glass door of the café grate on the sand as I open it. I can recall the smell of every hour. In the morning that of eggs frizzling in butter, the pungent cigarette, coffee and bad cognac; at five o'clock the fragrant odour of absinthe; and soon after the steaming soup ascends from the kitchen; and as the evening advances, the mingled smells of cigarettes, coffee, and weak beer . . . and it is there we sat and aestheticized till two o'clock in the morning."

And what did Moore learn? Daniel Halévy remembers that Stéphane Mallarmé would tell George Moore that he was gripped by the temptation to throw himself from the top of the Pont de L'Europe onto the tracks below, "in order to finally escape the mediocrity in which he was imprisoned." Most of the impressionist painters came here, including Manet, Monet, and the young Cézanne who was introduced by Zola. Diaz, Daubigny, and the aging Daumier also made appearances. From 1875 on, Sarah Bernhardt, who amused herself with sculpting in a nearby studio, was often seen at the Nouvelle-Athènes. Van Gogh, Lautrec, and Gauguin put in appearances here. Over beer or absinthe, they shared new ideas, forgot their woes, or just gossiped. As Moore wrote of this café: "though unacknowledged, though unknown, the influence of the Nouvelle-Athènes is inveterate in the artistic thought of the nineteenth century."

Montmartre was filled with cafés. Just a few streets away was the Brasserie des Martyrs, once a favorite of Baudelaire and Constantin Guy. Here Alphonse Daudet and Marie Rieu conducted a romance so passionate that Edmond de Goncourt described it as "a mad affair, drenched in absinthe and given a dramatic touch every now and then by a few knife-thrusts."

Then there was the Café du Rat Mort, popular with writers by day and lesbians by night. Another famous café was named after André Gill's painting of a leaping rabbit — Le Lapin à Gill — which became known as the Lapin Agile. Here the publicist Emil Goudeau had a literary club called the Hydropathes who regularly met to drink, sing, and read poetry. Nearby was the Chat Noir, owned by Théodore Salis, an unsuccessful painter who wanted to stage literary meetings. Though the Chat Noir opened in 1881, it claimed to date back to the reign of Julius Caesar. The surly waiters wore the formal garb of the Académie française, and Salis personally insulted each customer as he entered. Erik Satie played second piano here, and Alfred Jarry popped in occasionally. One of the Chat Noir regulars was Charles Cros, a linguistics scholar, mathematician, poet, and inventor (color photography process and a pre-Edison phonograph). Cros was a friend of Rimbaud and even loaned him an apartment. But according to Georges d'Esparbès, Cros drank twenty absinthes a day and died one night while finishing a last line of poetry. Such was the café life associated with absinthe.

When Degas's *L'Absinthe* was first exhibited in Brighton in 1876, it was simply titled *A Sketch of a French Café*. The critic for the *Brighton Gazette* called it: "The perfection of ugliness. . . . The color is as repulsive as the figures; a brutal sensual-looking French workman and a sickly-looking *grisette*; a most unlovely couple. The very disgusting novelty of the subject arrests attention. What there is to admire in it, is the skill of the artist, not the subject itself."

The critical sting in the review, however, did not encourage the Hill family to exhibit the picture again until the Hill auction at Christie's on February 20, 1892. Now titled *Figures at a Café*, the picture was hissed and booed off the easel. Had the absinthe glass been spotted? Undaunted, the Glasgow dealer Alexander Reid purchased the picture for 180 pounds and sold it shortly afterwards to the Glaswegian collector Arthur Kay.

A year later the picture was one of the 370 works in the exhibition titled "Painting and Sculpture by British and Foreign Artists of the Present Day" at the Grafton Gallery in London. The British group included Whistler, Watts, and Albert Moore (but not neo-impressionists Sickert and Steer); the foreign contingent included artists from Belgium, Norway, Sweden, Germany, and Italy; but it was dominated by French artists such as Raffaëlli, Besnard, Rodin, Fantin-Latour, and Degas. There was nothing particularly controversial about the show — no catalogue manifesto for instance — but now Degas's painting was provocatively titled, *L'Absinthe*.

At first the picture drew glowing praise. "A picture showing great power of rendering character and a superb use of material," said the *Glasgow Herald*. "Grim in its realism; incomparable in its art," wrote a critic for *The Star*. Even the conservative *Art Journal* was complimentary: "The

By Charles Cros

Avec les Fleurs, avec les Femmes,
Avec l'Absinthe, avec le Feu,
On peut se divertir un peu,
Jouer son rôle en quelque drame.

L'Absinthe, bue un soir d'hiver,
Eclaire en vert l'âme enfumée;
Et les Fleurs, sur la bien-aimée,
Embaument devant le Feu clair.

Puis, les baisers perdent leurs charmes,
Ayant duré quelques saisons;
Les reciproques trahisons
Font qu'on se quitte un jour sans larmes.

On brûle lettres et bouquets,
Et le Feu se met à l'alcôve;
Et si la triste vie est sauvé,
Reste l'Absinthe et ses hoquets . . .

Les portraits sont mangés de flammes . . .
Les doigts crispés sont tremblotants . . .
On meurt d'avoir dormi longtemps
Avec les Fleurs, avec les Femmes.

. . .

With Flowers, and with Women,
With Absinthe, and with this Fire,
We can divert ourselves awhile,
Act out our part in some drama.

Absinthe, on a winter evening,
Lights up in green the sooty soul;
And Flowers, on the beloved,
Grow fragrant before the clear Fire.

Later, kisses lose their charm
Having lasted several seasons;
And after mutual betrayals
We part one day without a tear.

We burn letters and bouquets.
And Fire takes our bower;
And if sad life is salvaged
Still there is Absinthe and its hiccups. . . .

The portraits are eaten by flames. . . .
Shriveled fingers tremble. . . .
We die from sleeping long
With Flowers, and with Women.

Charles Cros was poet, inventor, and
absinthe drinker. Photograph by Nadar.

characterization is complete, and what there is of
the story is set down with an absence of circumlocution that is almost painful."

Then, suddenly, a journalistic scuffle flared.
Critic D.S. MacColl started it when he devoted his
weekly column in the *Spectator* to covering the
exhibition and marveled at *L'Absinthe*. "The inex-
haustible picture, the one that draws you back,
and back again. . . . The subject, if you like, was
repulsive as you would have seen it, *before Degas
made it his*. If it appears so still, you may make up

Joris-Karl Huysmans, author of *À Rebours,* a novel celebrating decadence, wrote, "Even when made less offensive by a trickle of sugar, absinthe still reeks of copper, leaving on the palate a taste like a metal button slowly sucked."

your mind that the confusion and affliction from which you suffer are incurable."

Two weeks later, J.A. Spender, writing under a brash pseudonym, "The Philistine," rebutted MacColl in the *Westminster Gazette.* MacColl he challenged, "is not a critic so much as an advocate — the frankly partisan advocate of the young English imitators of the French Impressionists who call themselves the New English Art Club." Spender concluded: "If you have been taught to think that dignity of subject and the endeavor to portray a thing of beauty are the essence of art, you will never be induced to consider *L'Absinthe* a work of art, however 'incurable' your 'affliction and confusion' may be."

Suddenly, it was open season on Degas's picture. Sir William Blake Richmond, knight of Victorian principles, wrote, "The English Impressionists ridicule subject matter and 'literary art.' At the same time M. Degas is their god. Now *L'Absinthe* is a literary performance. It is not painting at all. It is a novelette — a treatise against drink.

Emile Zola photographed by Nadar. Although Zola's novel, *L'Assomoir*, was about alcoholism in general, there is one pertinent anecdote in it: "Boche had known a joiner who had stripped himself stark naked in the rue Saint-Martin and died doing the polka — he was an absinthe drinker."

Everything valuable about it could have been done, and has been done, by Zola. It would be ridiculous not to recognize M. Degas as a very clever man, but curiously enough his cleverness is literary more than pictorial."

Soon the exchange of letters (including a sensible suggestion from the artist Walter Sickert that they change the title and forget the whole business) came down to a struggle between the original combatants, MacColl and Richmond, in the April 15 issue of the *Spectator*. What was really at stake? There was the moral and teetotal view which saw the picture as a "temperance tract." But on a deeper level, the disagreement was really about the British view of French culture. Patriotic observers envisioned absinthe as "French poison" — no doubt in league with "the French disease," syphilis. In the past, attempts at a cultural "French connection" had been thwarted by British critics, and Baudelaire, his English disciple Swinburne, Zola and his intermediary George Moore, had all been attacked, vilified, and in some instances had their work banned.

Zola, in particular, was a topic of controversy in England because in 1885 and 1886 two of his novels (with prefaces by Moore) had been judged "immoral," resulting in the conviction of his English publisher Vizetelly. Zola had come to be a symbol of the decadent, even "obscene," happenings on the other side of the English Channel. Francophobia had already gained a voice in 1886 when John Trevor wrote a short tract entitled *French Art and English Morals* which warned against the establishment of a French "colony" in London. Without naming a single artist, he spoke of the "iniquitous realism" and his concern for "that high principle and healthy vigor, which alone can prevent our Art from being infected by the disease of this French School."

The English debate over his picture infuriated Degas. In the first place, as its owner Arthur Kay noted, "By error or devilment, the picture was not catalogued as *Au Café* but as *L'Absinthe*. I need hardly remark that Degas would never have given such a flamboyant title to a picture." Degas was angered by the publicity and embarrassed at being written about in the papers "like Whistler" (who thrived on controversy). And he was upset that his friends Ellen Andrée and Desboutin had their names connected with descriptions such as "vulgar," "ugly," and "besotted." But there was nothing he could do.

Still, why the furor over absinthe which was hardly drunk in England at all? The Zola controversy aside, one explanation would be the London publication just two years earlier in 1890 of Marie Corelli's novel, *Wormwood: A Drama of Paris*, which excoriated absinthe's evils. Corelli's intent is obvious in this passage from her introduction:

"The morbidness of the modern French mind is well-known and universally admitted, even by the French themselves; the open atheism, heartlessness, flippancy, and flagrant immorality of the whole modern French school of thought is unquestioned. . . . There are, no doubt, many causes for the wretchedly low standard of moral responsibility and fine feeling displayed by the Parisians of to-day — but I do not hesitate to say that one of those causes is undoubtedly the reckless Absinthemania, which pervades all classes, rich and poor alike."

The narrator of *Wormwood* is Gaston Beauvais, a well-bred young banker and amateur writer who is in love with Pauline, daughter of the Comte de Charmilles, an old friend of his father. Ah, what a marriage this would be! But, alas, Pauline's heart belongs to another — Silvion Guidèl, a saintly fellow from the provinces who is soon coming to Paris to claim her. Spurned, Gaston turns to the world of Bohemia and in a café encounters André Gessonex, a half-mad artist and absinthe drinker who introduces the naive Gaston to the Green Fairy.

Within a few days, Gaston becomes an absinthe addict. In the meantime, Silvion announces that he has decided to become a priest and cannot marry Pauline. Lucky Gaston catches her on the rebound. The wedding is announced even as Gaston is carrying on his affair with the Green Fairy:

"That night, the night before my wedding day, I drank deeply and long of my favorite nectar, — glass after glass I prepared, and drained each one off with insatiable and ever-increasing appetite — I drank till the solid walls of my own room, when at last I found myself there, appeared to me like transparent glass shot throughout with emerald flame. Surrounded on all sides by phantoms — beautiful, hideous, angelic, devilish — I reeled to my couch in a sort of waking swoon, conscious of strange sounds everywhere, like the clanging of brazen bells, and the silver fanfaronade of the trumpets of war, conscious too of a similar double sensation — namely, as though Myself were di-

vided into two persons, who opposed each other in a deadly combat, in which neither could possibly obtain even the merest shadow-victory!"

Gaston manages to get Pauline to the altar only to denounce her falsely as the mistress of the priestly Silvion. Pauline flees, and her shocked father, the comte, suddenly dies of shame. Gaston skulks away to become a nocturnal pariah, while Pauline disappears into the slums of Paris.

One night Gaston finds Silvion standing on a bridge sadly watching the moonlight on the Seine. Gaston strangles Silvion with the cords of his priest's habit and throws his body into the river. Days later, the bloated corpse is discovered. When the body is viewed at the morgue, the artist Gessonex morbidly marvels at the colors in the distorted, putrifying face while Gaston cackles with satisfaction.

Months later, when Gaston bumps into his father on the street, he boldly announces to the old man that he has become an *abinstheur*.

"An absintheur? You? What! You my son, a confessed slave to the abominable vice that not only makes of its votaries cowards but madmen? My God? Would you had died as a child, — would I had laid you in the grave, a little innocent lad as I remember you, than have lived to see you come to this. An absintheur! In that word is comprised all the worst possibilities of crime!"

Leaving his father, Gaston meets Gessonex for a drink in a café. They order absinthe and chat while Gessonex reads the daily paper. Here he finds he is the subject of an unflattering review of his latest work; without further ado, he whips out a pistol and shoots himself in the head. This "unpleasantness" *does* affect Gaston, but just a bit. The book ends with Gaston reflecting cynically over an absinthe: "And here I am, an absintheur in the City of Absinthe, and glory is neither for me, nor for thee Paris, thou frivolous, lovely, godless, lascivious dominion of Sin! Godless!"

Oscar Wilde, from his cell in Reading Gaol, commented with his usual acerbic wit on Corelli's writing style, "Now don't think I've anything against her moral character, but from the way she writes *she* ought to be here!"

Absinthe was not the only vice of the French. Drug use in general was infiltrating high society and becoming popular with women. Opium smoking had been introduced in the 1840s and 1850s by naval officers returning from the col-

From Marie Corelli's *Wormwood: A Drama of Paris,* 1890.

"Never tasted it!" exclaimed Gessonex amazedly. "Mon dieu! You a born and bred Parisian, have never tasted absinthe?"

I smiled at his excitement.

"Never! I have seen others drinking it often—but I have not liked the look of it somehow. A repulsive color to me, that medicinal green!"

He laughed a trifle nervously, and his hand trembled. But he gave no immediate reply, for at that moment the waiter placed a flacon of the drink in question on the table, together with the usual supply of water and tumblers. Carefully preparing and stirring the opaline mixture, Gessonex filled the glasses to the brim, and pushed one across to me. I made a faint sign of rejection. He laughed again in apparent amusement at my hesitation.

"By Venus and Cupid, and all the dear old heathen deities who are so remarkably convenient myths to take one's oath upon," he said. "I hope you will not compel me to consider you a fool, Beauvais! What an idea that is of yours—'medicinal green!' Think of melted emeralds instead! There, beside you, you have the most marvelous cordial in all the world—drink and you will find your sorrows transmuted—yourself transformed! Even if no better result be obtained than escaping the chill you have incurred in this night's heavy drenching, that is surely enough! Life without absinthe! I cannot imagine it! For me it would be impossible! I should hang, drown or shoot myself into infinitude, out of sheer rage at the continued cruelty and injustice of the world—but with this divine nectar of Olympus I can defy misfortune and laugh at poverty, as though they were the merest bagatelles! Come!—to your health, mon brave! Drink with me!"

"He raised his glass glimmering pallidly in the light,—his words, his manner, fascinated me, and a curious thrill ran through my brains. There was something spectral in his expression too, as though the skeleton of the man had become suddenly visible beneath its fleshly covering—as though Death had for a moment peered through the veil of Life . . ."

Marie Corelli (1855–1924) author of the histrionic novel *Wormwood: A Drama of Paris.*

onies, and morphine arrived as a painkiller in the 1870 war, leaving many veterans addicted. Eugen Weber noted in his book, *France: Fin de Siècle:* "Fashionable circles soon took it up; novelists wrote about it; society ladies got together to exchange injections; jewelers did a thriving trade in silver-gilt or gold-plated syringes; and Alexander Dumas the younger declared, 'Morphine is the absinthe of women.'"

Maurice Talmeyr, author of *Les Possédés de la morphine,* told the story of a young vicomte who, during a fashionable dinner party suddenly rolls up the sleeve of his dinner jacket and gives himself an injection with an enameled syringe; to make things even racier, the young vicomte turns out to be a lesbian dressed as a man. "Addiction, homosexuality and transvestism did not necessar-

ily go together," notes Weber, "but they moved in the same circles and were part of the same fin de siècle spirit."

There were plenty of other drugs to choose from. Guy de Maupassant preferred ether and introduced it to fashionable circles where strawberries soaked in ether were considered a refined dessert. Cocaine was also catching on, thanks to doctors such as Sigmund Freud who at first mistook it for a miracle drug against depression. Sarah Bernhardt appeared in advertising art for Vin Coca Mariani, a medicinal wine containing an infusion of coca leaves, while Marcel Proust was addicted to camphor cigarettes.

The trend to drugs was not just confined to France. Marie Corelli, in her introduction to *Wormwood*, wrote: "It must also be remembered that in the many French *cafés* and restaurants which have recently sprung up in London, Absinthe is always to be obtained at its customary low price, — French habits, French fashions, French books, French pictures, are particularly favored by the English, and who can predict that French drug-taking shall not also become

à la mode in Britain? — particularly at a period when our medical men are bound to admit that the love of Morphia is fast becoming almost a mania with hundreds of English women!"

Ironically, though Degas's painting, *L'Absinthe*, became an icon of the absinthe age, Ellen Andrée hardly ever drank absinthe and lived a long and happy life. She never became as famous on the stage as she had once hoped, but she remained one of the few female regulars at La Nouvelle-Athènes. Being pegged as a heavy absinthe drinker irked her, however, and in 1921, Madame Andrée decided to put the matter straight. Interviewed during intermission in her loge at the Edouard VII theater, she said, "My glass was filled with absinthe. Desboutin has something quite innocuous in his . . . and we look like two idiots," she told critic Félix Fénéon. "I didn't look bad at the time, I can say that today; I had an air about me that your Impressionists thought 'quite modern,' I had chic and I could hold the pose as they wanted me to . . . But Degas — didn't he slaughter me!"

Toulouse-Lautrec (*left*) and Lucien
Métivet, another poster artist, drinking
absinthe in Lautrec's studio, circa 1887.

Chapter 5

From Montmartre to the Marquesas: Lautrec, Van Gogh, Monticelli, and Gauguin

The symbolist painter Gustave Moreau once remarked of Henri de Toulouse-Lautrec's genius, "His paintings were entirely painted in absinthe." A lurid hallucinatory glow emanates from Lautrec's pictures of dance halls and houses of ill-repute — as if alcohol and libidinous longing had heightened the perceptions of both artist and subject. Lautrec painted Montmartre as a smorgasbord of amateur and professional sin, a place to lose one's self for a night or a lifetime.

Lautrec was known for carrying absinthe in a hollow cane when he prowled seedy dance halls like the Moulin Rouge. "One should drink little . . . but often," Lautrec would tell his friends. A great connoisseur of absinthe cocktails, he tested home-made concoctions on his friends "in the manner of the Borgias," said one biographer. His favorite recipe, created for Yvette Guilbert, was called *tremblement de terre* (earthquake) and consisted of absinthe and cognac.

Lautrec was not the only one to serve absinthe in different ways. Depending on the café or your taste, you could have it à la hussarde, la purée, l'amazone, la vichy, la bourgeoise (also called la panachée), or gommée. Absinthe minuit was served with white wine instead of water and absinthe de vidangeur (scavenger absinthe) was

absinthe mixed with red wine according to the famed singer Aristide Bruant (immortalized in Lautrec's poster as the man with the red scarf and black hat).

With absinthe on so many artistic tongues, it soon became part of the language. In 1878, "avaler ton absinthe" (swallow your absinthe) meant to swallow one's pride or to "eat crow," while by 1901, "renverser ton absinthe" (upset your absinthe) meant "to kick the bucket." "Demander ton absinthe" meant to "ask to put in your two bits" and "faire l'absinthe" meant to "accidentally spit on someone while talking."

When Lautrec wasn't observing the prostitutes in brothels or dancers at the Moulin Rouge, he spent his time in the Café Weber, which was popular with sportsmen, writers, and painters. If he found it too crowded, he headed next door to the Irish and American Bar, which was a hangout for hardened drinkers who sat in silent contemplation of their bottles. The bar was tended by Randolphe, a half-breed of Chinese and American blood, who could mix absinthe with uncanny dexterity into layered cocktails called "Night Cups" or "Rainbow Cups." Frequently the last client to leave the bar, Lautrec would hail a coachman to drive him to the Avenue Frochot

Lautrec's *Monsieur Boileau at the Café*,
1893, is a portrait of a bon vivant killing
time with a cigarette, a glass of absinthe,
and a game of dominoes. Little is known
about Boileau, but the white-bearded
man in top hat in the background is the
artist's father.

Lautrec's *Still Life with Billiards* has an innocent enough title, but the glass on the left holds absinthe.

Henri de Toulouse-Lautrec's *Absinthe Drinker*, 1888.

Toulouse-Lautrec's Paris by night.

where he could sleep in the carriage until morning. Lautrec's father, Comte Alphonse de Toulouse-Lautrec, heartily disapproved of his son's life. Upon hearing that Lautrec had been seen drunk on many occasions, he grunted, "Why doesn't he go to England? They scarcely notice the drunks there."

One day in early March 1899, Lautrec awoke from an evening of intoxication to find himself in an unfamiliar room. The door was padlocked and the windows barred while at the foot of his bed stood a male nurse. He was in the Chateau Saint-James, a beautiful eighteenth-century mansion situated at the edge of the Bois de Boulogne which had been transformed into an asylum. In February, after he had suffered an aggravated attack of delirium tremens, his close friend Doctor Bourges and his cousin Gabriel Tapié de Céleyran had convinced Lautrec's parents that they should commit Lautrec to the sanitorium to undergo a cure for alcoholism. He had been kidnapped while delirious outside his studio by two male nurses.

Lautrec was terrified of ending his days in confinement. Ten years earlier, looking at an engraving of a madman by caricaturist André Gill (a heavy absinthe drinker himself who died in an asylum), Lautrec had said to his friend Gauzi,

"That's what awaits us all." In terror he wrote to his father to release him. "Papa, now you have the opportunity to behave like a good man. I am imprisoned, and all that is imprisoned, dies!"

Instead, Lautrec's father took the advice of the physicians and left him where he was. The first medical examination revealed evidence of hallucination and amnesia, accepted as typical symptoms of the heavy absinthe drinker. The prognosis was not encouraging. Desperate, Lautrec hit on an idea. If he could jog his memory, they would have to let him out, wouldn't they? He began to draw and paint, and gradually the line and color brought back whole sections of his life — a visit to the circus, a day at the beach with friends. He was released in late May. Though he carefully refrained from absinthe and other alcohol, his health declined. He died at home in 1901, leaving behind the most telling record of Paris's underbelly and the world of absinthe.

In 1887, Toulouse-Lautrec drew a pastel portrait of his friend Vincent Van Gogh musing over a glass of absinthe. Lautrec and Gauguin had introduced the monkish but volatile Dutchman to absinthe and prostitutes — de rigueur vices for a true Bohemian. Though Van Gogh never quite fit into any society, he became a regular at the

Lautrec sketched this pastel portrait of
Van Gogh drinking absinthe in a café
about 1887. Van Gogh became a regular
at the Café du Tambourin, where the
neo-impressionists congregated.

Van Gogh's painting of an absinthe glass and water decanter. Like all of his still lifes, it is a self-portrait.

Café du Tambourin where many of the neo-impressionist painters such as Lautrec, Bernard, and Anquetin congregated and exhibited their paintings.

Van Gogh's sad existence has undoubtedly been the subject of more conjecture than any other artist's life. Not only art historians but doctors have wondered why his paintings were characterized by intense yellow hues and halo effects. Chronic solar injury, glaucoma, and even cataracts have been suggested, while some physicians believed that Van Gogh had acute mania with generalized delirium. Others diagnosed epilepsy, and in 1981, Dr. Thomas Courtney Lee concluded that Van Gogh may have suffered from digitalis intoxication.

Digitalis, derived from the foxglove plant, was a common remedy in the nineteenth century for epilepsy. In large doses it can produce disorientation, yellow vision, and even coronas of swirling light. That would fit Van Gogh's late paintings which are dominated by yellow, a chromatic obsession he described at length in his letters. But there is no record that Van Gogh was ever treated with digitalis. The only fact rising above conjecture is that Van Gogh drank enormous amounts of absinthe.

Van Gogh painted a still life of an absinthe bottle and glass in 1886, and like all of his still lifes, it was a form of self-portraiture. Van Gogh was not happy in Paris and feared that Bohemian vices were destroying him as an artist. On Lautrec's advice, he headed south to Arles. It was winter when he arrived, but spring came early to Provence and the sun and cherry blossoms made the countryside seem as exotic as the Orient to the pale, stoic Dutchman.

"Must I tell you the truth," he wrote to his brother Theo, "and add that the zouaves, the brothels, the adorable little Arlesiennes going to their first Communion, the priest in his surplice, who looks like a dangerous rhinoceros, the people that drink absinthe, all seem to me creatures from another world." It is the first, but not the last time Vincent mentions absinthe in his letters. In his first months in the south, Van Gogh restrained his intake of absinthe and prostitutes because of a stomach condition which he blamed on the bad wine of Paris. "I was certainly going the right way for a stroke when I left Paris," he wrote to Theo on May 4, 1888. "I paid for it nicely afterward! When I stopped drinking, when I stopped smoking

so much, when I began to think again instead of trying not to think — Good Lord, the depression and prostration of it."

Van Gogh blamed his depressions not only on the excesses he had indulged in Paris but on his genes. As he wrote to Theo: "My poor boy, our neurosis, etc. comes it's true from our way of living, which is purely the artist's life but it is also a fatal inheritance, since in civilization the weakness increases from generation to generation." His mother's sister had epilepsy, his sister Wilhelmina ended her life in a psychiatric ward, and his other brother, Cornelis, purportedly committed suicide. Theo himself would die insane just a year after Vincent.

A great influence on Van Gogh was the Marseilles artist Adolphe Joseph Thomas Monticelli, who died while Vincent was still living in Montmartre. The two artists never met, but Theo had some of Monticelli's paintings for sale and Vincent greatly admired their jewel-like colors and thickly encrusted surfaces. He was also troubled by the rumors that Monticelli had died of absinthe consumption and wrote about it to Theo: "While I think of it, I want to tell you that more and more I doubt the truth of the legend of Monticelli drinking such enormous quantities of absinthe. When I look at his work, I can't think it possible that a man who was flabby with drink could have done that."

The reports of Monticelli's café life and absinthe drinking are certainly obscured by legend, but by most accounts he was a heavy consumer. Monticelli usually drank at the Café de l'Univers in Marseilles, whose proprietor, César Boyer, bought Monticelli's work and never tired of promoting his talent or filling his glass. Monticelli would sell a couple of paintings as he made his rounds of the cafés — and then drink the proceeds.

Monticelli was a dreamer, a placid, good-natured man who, after a religious faltering in his youth, fell into a kind of aesthetic mysticism. He painted voluptuous canvases of nymphs, Don Quixote, and Faustus. Verlaine, who bought a Monticelli painting in 1870, once remarked, "here is a painter that I would like to meet, to ask him if he would lend me his eyes and tell me his dreams."

Van Gogh was strongly affected by Monticelli's work and by the character of the man he perceived behind those visionary pictures. In his letters to Theo and friends, he mentions Monticelli's name some fifty times, writing, "I am sure that I am a

An early self-portrait by Adolphe Monticelli. Van Gogh was alarmed by rumors of Monticelli's absinthe drinking.

Jules Monge's 1884 portrait of Monticelli was also titled *L'Absinthe*. One biographer recounted, "Monticelli would tip-toe furtively into the street, duck into the Café Plauchet in the alley across from la Fontaine, where at that hour there were only a few customers. He would slip onto a bench in a dark corner there, head back, eyes ecstatic, sip in little mouthfuls of his Ambrosia (translation: absinthe)." This picture was recently stolen from a private collection in Paris.

The Drinker, by Monticelli, shows
the impasto style that influenced
Van Gogh's art.

continuation of him here, as if I was his son or his brother." In fact Van Gogh pledged himself to carry on in painting where Monticelli had left off.

"I so often think of Monticelli," wrote Van Gogh, "and when my mind dwells on the stories going around about his death, it seems to me that not only must you exclude the idea of his dying a drunkard in the sense of being besotted by drink, but you must realize that here as a matter of course one spends one's life in the open air and in cafés far more than in the North. My friend the postman, for instance, lives a great deal in cafés, and is certainly more or less a drinker, and has been so all his life. But he is so much the reverse of a sot, his exaltation is so natural, so intelligent, and he argues with such sweep, in the style of Garibaldi, that I gladly reduce the legend of Monticelli the drunkard on absinthe to exactly the same proportions as my postman's."

Van Gogh had several months of good painting in the summer of 1888. But painting alone under the burning sun gave him a thirst and a loneliness which drove him to cafés. In September he painted a favorite haunt of absinthe drinkers and derelicts, the Café de l'Alcazar. "In my painting of the 'Night Café,' I have tried to express the idea that a café is a place where a man can ruin oneself, go mad, commit a crime. So I have tried to express, as it were, the powers of darkness in a low public house, by soft Louis XV green and malachite, contrasting with yellow-green and harsh blue-greens, and all this in an atmosphere like a devil's furnace, of pale sulphur." In short, the color of absinthe.

That same month Gauguin arrived to share a house with Van Gogh. He, too, painted a picture of the Café de l'Alcazar. Within a few weeks, the two artists quarreled, and Van Gogh went back to absinthe drinking. Gauguin, a frank but often self-serving source of art history, reported the following episode:

"That same evening we went into a café. He ordered a light absinthe. Suddenly he flung the glass and its contents into my face. I managed to

Van Gogh's *Night Café at Arles*, 1888, has an unsettling psychological pull on the viewer. As Van Gogh wrote, "I have tried to express the idea that a café is a place where a man can ruin oneself, go mad, commit a crime."

Paul Gauguin's *Dans un café à Arles*
depicts the same café Van Gogh
painted. The proprietress sits before a
tall glass of absinthe, with water siphon
and sugar cubes at the ready. In the
background sit Van Gogh's postman-
friend and a trio of prostitutes.

duck and grab him, take him out of the café and
across the Place Victor Hugo. A few minutes later,
Vincent was in his own bed and in a matter of
seconds had fallen asleep, not to awaken until
morning.

"When he awoke he was perfectly calm and
said to me: 'My dear Gauguin, I have a dim
recollection that I offended you last night.'"

Three days later, on Christmas Eve 1888, Gauguin was walking in the street when he heard
footsteps behind him and turned to see Van Gogh
coming at him with a razor. Gauguin reported that

he "stared him to a halt" and Van Gogh retreated. Later that night Van Gogh cut off the lobe of his left ear, put it in an envelope, and gave it to a brothel wench named Rachel with these words: "Guard this object carefully." Van Gogh stumbled home, closed the shutters, and lighted a lamp near his window. He wrapped his bloodstained body in his bedsheets and passed out. Gauguin spent the night at a hotel and returned to the apartment in the morning to find it infested by police who asked him: "What have you done to your friend?" They pointed to Van Gogh's lifeless body wrapped in the bloody sheets.

"What do you mean?"

"Come, come. You know perfectly well what we mean. He's dead."

Van Gogh was not dead, and when he came to, he was taken to the hospital. Gauguin decided it was a good time to leave the Dutchman to his madness.

By New Year's, Van Gogh seemed to have completely recovered and was released. He painted several masterpieces that winter and even visited the recipient of his ear at the brothel, writing to Theo on February 3, 1889: "Yesterday I went to see the girl I had gone to when I was out of my wits. They told me that in this country things like that are not out of the ordinary."

On February 9, Van Gogh suffered a relapse and was re-admitted to the asylum. He was beset by unearthly sounds and voices and believed that someone was trying to poison him. Released again, he found that many of the citizens of Arles actively disliked him. Children mocked him and threw pebbles at him; adults laughed at him when he painted outside at night with candles strapped to the brim of his hat. It did not help him to learn that some eighty townspeople had signed a petition asking that he be confined. Admitted to the asylum and then released once more, he was lonely and friendless, when he wrote to his brother on April 30, 1889:

"If I were without your friendship, they would remorselessly drive me to suicide, and however cowardly I am, I should end by doing it. There, as you will see, I hope, is the juncture where it is permissible for us to protest against society and defend ourselves. You can be fairly sure that the Marseilles artist [Monticelli] who committed suicide did not in any way do it as the result of absinthe, for the simple reason that no one would have offered it to him and he couldn't have had anything to buy it with. Besides he would drink it,

Paul Gauguin drank absinthe in Paris, in Arles with Van Gogh, and in Tahiti.

L'ABSINTHE

By Raoul Ponchon

Absinthe, je t'adore, certes!
Il me semble, quand je te bois,
Humer l'âme des jeunes bois,
Pendant la belle saison verte!

Ton frais parfum me déconcerte
Et dans ton opale je vois
Des cieux habités autrefois,
Comme par une porte ouverte.

Qu'importe, ô recours des maudits!
Que tu sois un vain paradis,
Si tu contentes mon envie;

Et si, devant que j'entre au port,
Tu me fais supporter la vie,
En m'habituant à la mort.

. . .

Absinthe, I adore you, truly!
It seems, when I drink you,
I inhale the young forest's soul,
During the beautiful green season.

Your perfume disconcerts me
And in your opalescence
I see the full heavens of yore,
As through an open door.

What matter, O refuge of the damned!
That you a vain paradise be,
If you appease my need;

And if, before I enter the door,
You make me put up with life,
By accustoming me to death.

Raoul Ponchon drew this self-portrait
with a beer mug; nevertheless, he wrote
a half-dozen poems about absinthe.

68

Poet Gustave Kahn (1859–1936), self-styled inventor of free verse.

ABSINTHE

By Gustave Kahn

Absinthe, mère des bonheurs, ô liqueur infinie, tu miroites en mon verre comme les yeux verts et pâles de la maîtresse qu jadis j'aimais. Absinthe, mère des bonheurs, comme Elle, tu laisses dans le corps un souvenir de lointaines douleurs; absinthe, mère des rages folles et des ivresses titubantes, ou l'on peut, sans se croire un fou, se dire aimé de sa maîtresse. Absinthe, ton parfum me berce. . . .

. . .

Absinthe, mother of all happiness, O infinite liquor, you glint in my glass green and pale like the eyes of the mistress I once loved. Absinthe, mother of happiness, like Her, you leave in the body a memory of distant pain; absinthe, mother of insane rages and of staggering drunkenness, where one can say without thinking oneself mad that one is loved by one's mistress. Absinthe, your fragrance soothes me. . . .

not solely for pleasure, but because, being ill already, he needed it to keep him going."

Incredibly, Van Gogh seems to be writing about his own relationship with absinthe rather than Monticelli's. Monticelli was popular in the cafés, and as Jules Monge said, he sold plenty of paintings. Van Gogh was just the opposite. Unpopular, unsociable, he only sold two pictures in his life.

Fauvist painter Paul Signac visited Van Gogh that spring and reported: "Returning after spending the whole day in the blazing sun, in the torrid heat, and having no real home in town, he would take his seat on the terrace of a café. And the absinthes and brandies would follow each in quick succession."

After Vincent tried to drink a quart of turpentine in his studio, he was sent to the asylum at Saint-Rémy on May 7, 1889. The doctors began to treat him with hydrotherapy for acute mania and epilepsy. A century later, a precise diagnosis of Van Gogh's illness is still unavailable, despite hundreds of conjectures.

But we do know a few facts: Van Gogh suffered from syphilis contracted from prostitutes off the docks at Antwerp; there was also a history of mental illness in his family. Some physicians now believe that Van Gogh may have had a congenital brain lesion that was aggravated by absinthe.

As his attacks occurred with greater frequency, Van Gogh fell into despair for fear of becoming totally mad. On July 27, 1890, he took stock of his condition and shot himself in the stomach. It took him two days to die; he was only thirty-seven.

On the other side of the world, Van Gogh's former roommate in Arles, Paul Gauguin, was living in Tahiti with a fifteen-year-old wife. It sounds like paradise if you ignore the facts: Gauguin suffered from syphilis and eczema; he painted pictures few of the colonials liked; and the local priests advised their Tahitian Catholic flock not to associate with him due to the "indecent" nature of his art. Gauguin despised most of the French civilians who, in turn, disliked him. But when good news came in the form of a 1,200 franc check from his Paris dealer, Gauguin was euphoric and wrote a friend on January 18, 1897, "I sit at my door, smoking a cigarette and sipping my absinthe, and I enjoy every day without a care in the world."

69

Alfred Jarry leaving his house at Corbeil for Paris. He loved the bicycle, admiring the way it melded man and machine. But best of all he loved absinthe, which he called "holy water."

Chapter 6

Jarry and Picasso: The Absinthe Blur of Art

By the 1890s, absinthe had long outgrown its cult status and was drunk by millions. Yet certain artists and writers continued to treat it as a personal obsession. The surrealist André Breton later remarked, "Poe est surrealist dans l'aventure, Baudelaire est surrealist dans la morale, Jarry est surrealist dans absinthe."

Alfred Jarry, author of the avant-garde play *Ubu roi*, had the definitive fascination for absinthe. He was obsessed with the idea of total abandonment to the hallucinatory world of dreams. Like Rabelais, Jarry proclaimed a faith in alcohol and called absinthe "holy water," "essence of life," and "sacred herb." He drank defiantly and triumphantly, believing that alcohol released man's true potential, a credo that aligned him more closely with Rimbaud than with Baudelaire.

With his typical absurdist logic, Jarry wrote: "Anti-alcoholics are unfortunates in the grip of water, that terrible poison, so solvent and corrosive that out of all substances it has been chosen for washing and scourings, and a drop of water, added to a clear liquid like absinthe, muddies it." For that reason, Jarry chose to drink absinthe straight. By remaining in a constant twilight state induced by absinthe and ether, he gradually broke down the barriers between his own personality and the bizarre character of his imagination, Père Ubu.

Jarry's notorious play *Ubu roi* made him a widely imitated cult figure at the age of twenty-three. It tells the story of Père Ubu, a pear-shaped boor who murders his way to the throne of Poland. After pillaging the country, he is defeated by the son of the former king who drives him to France; here the munificent Père Ubu, possessed by absurd logic, promises to do the same for the French.

In *Ubu roi*, Jarry turned theater into flagrant confrontation with the audience. A tour de force publicity effort packed opening night of the play, but few of the spectators were prepared for the first word spoken on stage by Père Ubu: *"Merdre!"* (the extra "r" made the exclamation the equivalent of screaming "Shite!"). It sent the audience into an uproar, and the play was delayed fifteen minutes. The rest of the drama was filled with slapstick and provocation — just as Jarry's own life would be.

Jarry arrived in Paris at the age of seventeen in 1891 and soon became a part of the Tuesday night literary circle that met at poet Stéphane Mallarmé's. There he met the editors of the *Mercure*

Père Ubu in Paris by Bonnard.

Véritable portrait de Monsieur Ubu

The definitive Père Ubu in a woodblock
by Jarry.

Theater announcement for *Ubu roi*,
woodcut by Jarry.

de France and the general staff of the symbolist
movement such as Rémy de Gourmont, Gustave
Kahn, and others less well known at the time,
including Paul Valéry, André Gide, and Maurice
Ravel. But none caused as much sensation as Jarry
who, wrote novelist Madame Rachilde, had the
"eyes of a nightbird," and made his literary debut
"like a wild animal entering the ring."

Jarry's life was eccentric in every way, from his
living habits and attire to his odd-sounding voice.
He spoke in a strangely clipped circumlocution,
referring to his bicycle as "that which rolls," and
derived most of his nourishment by angling in the
Seine for "that which swims." He ate his meals in
reverse: dessert first, soup last. Like Baudelaire
who once dyed his hair green, Jarry painted his
face and hands green, the color of absinthe. Jarry
usually attired himself in the garb of a bicycle
racer: tight sweater, short coat, and old trousers
tucked into his socks. Occasionally, he wore a
paper shirt with a trompe l'oeil bow tie painted on
it in India ink. Once, finding himself without shoes
to wear to Mallarmé's funeral, he borrowed some
yellow high-heels from Rachilde who wore the
same size.

In Paris, Jarry often carried pistols on his
absinthe-drinking rounds and once in a café he
tried to shoot a cigar out of a man's mouth. When
a stranger stopped him on the street to ask directions, Jarry whipped out his pistol and told the
terrified man to pose his questions from six feet
away.

Jarry was a famous misogynist and probably an
inactive homosexual. The only woman whose
company he could tolerate — and perhaps vice
versa — was the novelist Rachilde, whose husband, Alfred Vallette, published Jarry's work in
the *Mercure de France*. Years after Jarry's death,
Rachilde described his drinking habits in a book
called *Alfred Jarry: Supermale of Letters*:

"He would start off the day by absorbing two
liters of white wine. Three absinthes would be
spaced out between ten and noon, then at luncheon he would wash down his fish or beefsteak
with red or white wine alternating with further
absinthes. In the afternoon, a few coffees forti-
fied with marcs or other spirits whose names I
forget, then at dinner — after, it goes without
saying, more apéritifs — he could still withstand
two or more bottles of wine of any vintage, good
or bad. And yet I never saw him really drunk but
once, when I set to shooting off his revolvers
which sobered him instantly."

Jarry sniffed ether, because, he said, "Ça détache." Jarry also detached himself from the ordinary through the speed of machines. "Fueling one's mind with crushed, confused fragments relieves the memory's secret dungeons of their destructive work, and after such an assimilation the mind can more readily re-create entirely original forms and colors." He loved the way a bicycle blended man and machine in motion.

Jarry's humor was notorious. Once while attending the funeral of a well-known scholar, he watched as solemn and gowned academicians filed past the bier paying their last respects. Then in a metallic voice, he inquired of the audience at large, "Would someone be so kind as to inform us? Which one is the corpse?"

On another occasion, at a garden luncheon at Rachilde's country house, he pulled out his pistol and began shooting off the tops of champagne bottles lined up on the garden wall. His hostess's neighbor arrived in hysterics, shouting that Jarry was endangering the lives of her children. With typical sangfroid, Jarry assured her, "Should an accident befall any of them, Madame, we should be pleased to help you produce others."

Jarry kept owls, first alive and later stuffed, which he admired for the strange shape of their beaks and their nocturnal habits which resembled his own. When his parents died leaving him a little money, he moved to an apartment on the Boulevard Saint-Germain which he equipped with a little marionette theater to entertain his guests. He moved again to 7 Rue Cassette, an apartment with such a low ceiling that his friend Guillaume Apollinaire reported that the only food that could be comfortably eaten there was a flounder. Jarry, as it happened, served almost nothing but fish and absinthe to the rare visitors to his equally unusual summer residence, an old stable for barge mules on the Coudray docks south of Paris.

Paul Chauveau, Jarry's biographer, wrote that absinthe for Jarry was "more than a habit, a vice or a weakness. It was a conviction, a need, a sure way of attaining the absolute. At first Jarry drank to scandalize, continued for the sake of continuing, then out of despair, pride and genius." When absinthe became too costly, he switched to ether.

In his novel, *Les Jours et les nuits*, Jarry depicted the possibility of "true hallucination," the sustained waking dream in which there is no distinguishing between night and day. His absinthe drinking was part of this plan to so alter life and

Jarry by Bonnard.

Jarry by Picasso.

Jarry by Félix Vallotton.

73

A puppet of Père Ubu made by Jarry.

art that they fused. While it would be impossible to determine scientifically how absinthe — as distinct from other alcohols — contributed to Jarry's literature or mental state, the drink had an artificial quality that appealed to Jarry.

Jarry actually considered his greatest achievement to be *Gestes et opinions du docteur Faustroll, 'Pataphysician* (Exploits and Opinions of Dr. Faustroll, 'Pataphysician). In this book, published after his death, Jarry invented the science of 'Pataphysics (complete with Greek apostrophe) which, according to Anthony West, dealt with "the laws governing the exception; it was the science of imaginary solutions." The book follows the curious Dr. Faustroll who, accompanied by a baboon and a summons-server, travels over dry land in a sieve in search of 'pataphysical solutions. In the end, Dr. Faustroll moves into eternity, having proved geometrically that God equals the tangential point between Zero and Infinity.

By 1906, the thirty-four-year-old Jarry's absinthe habits had indeed driven him to the tangential point of life and infinity, but not necessarily to God. As Rachilde wrote, "He savored the joy of martyrdom when he drank absinthe, knowing perfectly well that he was killing himself." A month before his death in 1906, Jarry wrote Rachilde a letter not only predicting but welcoming his end, saying that Père Ubu, "believes that the brain, in its decomposition, functions beyond death and that it is *his dreams* that are paradise." After surviving a major alcoholic crisis thanks to his sister's care at a country house, he returned to Paris. Here he was stricken with tubercular meningitis and remained semi-conscious in his room for several days before being discovered by friends. At the hospital he lapsed into a coma and recovered momentarily before death to croak a last request: not for absinthe, nor for a priest, but for something absurdly normal . . . a toothpick.

As André Breton wrote: "Beginning with Jarry, much more than with Wilde, the differentiation long held to be necessary between art and life has been challenged, to wind up annihilated in its principle." Jarry lived in a time of great changes in art, society, and politics. No wonder the symbolist poets and later the surrealists were attracted to anarchism. As Jerrold Seigel notes, the radical symbolist poet Pierre Quillard described art itself as an engine of social liberation, whether its subject matter was politically oriented or not. "Whoever communicates to his brothers in suffering the secret splendor of his dreams acts upon the

Jarry by Frédérick-August Cazals, 1897.

surrounding society in the manner of a solvent, and makes of all those who understand him, often without their realization, outlaws and rebels."

Absinthe, too, was seen as a "solvent" on society. By the time Pablo Picasso began painting absinthe drinkers in 1900, the Green Fairy's reputation had so declined that it was openly called "bottled madness" and "the green curse." Temperance groups, politicians, and doctors raged against a poison they believed was enslaving the French population.

Picasso was highly influenced by Alfred Jarry and for a time drank absinthe, played the dandy, and carried a revolver. But unlike the inventor of Père Ubu, Picasso never damaged his own health.

Not a heavy drinker himself, Picasso was fascinated by the world of absinthe, and his early pictures of Paris by night have some of Lautrec's jaded aspect.

Born in Malaga in 1881, Picasso spent his youth in Barcelona, Spain's most avante-garde city, but traveled to Paris in October 1900 with fellow artist Carlos Casagemas. Soon the two Spaniards were part of the Montmartre crowd, painting or writing in cold tenement studios and frequenting the Moulin de la Galette. Picasso was befriended by Max Jacob, the poet, and was even given a show by Ambroise Vollard, the famous art dealer who represented Cézanne. All went well until the night of February 17, 1901, when Casagemas shot himself in the back room of a wineshop. This single event seemed to crystalize Picasso's own sense of failure, driving him to paint in blue and green, the colors of absinthe. Picasso returned to Barcelona where for the next two years he painted beggars, blind guitarists, and prostitutes, the haunting pictures of his Blue Period.

Pablo Picasso in 1904, just after ending the Blue Period.

La Taverne Pousset, a café on the Boulevard des Italiens, as Picasso would have found it in 1900.

Picasso's *Woman Drinking Absinthe*,
1901.

Picasso's *The Absinthe Drinker*, 1901, is a powerful psychological portrait of addiction.

Picasso's *Two Women Seated in A Bar,*
1902, was painted in Barcelona.

Picasso was only twenty when he created the magnificent *Woman Drinking Absinthe.* It is an intensely psychological picture of a person under the influence of alcohol. The long arms and sinewy hands enfold her meager body while her eyes glow with what may be carnal contemplation. Before her sits the absinthe. In the mirror behind, the images of the outside world flatten and change form.

With the exception of Degas's *L'Absinthe,* most of the early depictions of absinthe drinkers in art were male; the exceptions were advertising posters of coy maidens proffering a healthy elixir. But by the fin de siècle, absinthe pictures showed a growing number of women, and they were no longer depicted as healthy, happy, or virtuous. Doctors

and social observers alike saw absinthe as a vice peculiarly attractive to women.

As one absinthe expert, Dr. J.A. Laborde, wrote in 1903: "Woman has a particular taste for absinthe and if she intoxicates herself rarely with wine and alcohol, it has to be recognized that in Paris at least, she is frequently attracted by *les apéritifs* and, without risk of exaggeration, I would say that this intoxication has been for several years as common among women as among men. It is possible to state that clear cases of chronic absinthism occur in women at the end of eight, ten months, or a year in young women and even young girls of eighteen to twenty years old."

In Picasso's other pictures of this time, gaunt prostitutes and idle dandies stare out at the world

Picasso's watercolor, *The Poet Cornutti*, 1902–1903, is sometimes titled *Absinthe*. Max Jacob, a close friend of Picasso, wrote a note on the back of the watercolor explaining that Cornutti, an ether addict like himself, had died in obscurity, probably from malnutrition.

with glazed eyes set in pallid, bloodless faces, as if overcome by the experience of city life. Already there are hints of the distortion and symbolism that would characterize Picasso's later work. With their cloisonné divisions and dark outlines, these pictures are more emblems of feeling than depictions of nature. Unlike impressionist paintings such as Degas's *L'Absinthe*, Picasso's pictures are no longer "a slice of life" — they seem to express the emotional world within the artist.

Picasso returned from Barcelona to Paris in 1904 and moved into the dilapidated studio building at 13 Rue Ravignan, christened the *Bateau-Lavoir* (laundry barge) by Max Jacob. Nearby, at the foot of Montmartre, was the Cirque Médrano, the circus which Picasso visited three or four times a week with friends. Almost immediately, he fell in love with Fernande Olivier, the former mistress of a sculptor who had gone mad. The Blue Period ended and the Rose Period was in full bloom. Picasso met Gertrude Stein, who became an early

patron, and the poet Guillaume Apollinaire, who inspired Picasso with his unconventional poetry and promoted his art through criticism.

Beginning in 1906, Picasso's work changed dramatically — so much so that even Apollinaire and Jacob found nothing to praise. Gertrude Stein's brother Leo commented, "You've been trying to paint the fourth dimension. How amusing!" In a few short months, Picasso had demolished conventional perspective. Even the fauvist painter Georges Braque had a hard time accepting Picasso's famous picture, *Les Demoiselles d'Avignon*. But over the next two years, working on landscapes in separate locations, both artists found themselves re-examining Cézanne's geometry. When they discovered their mutual interest, they worked together "like roped mountaineers" as Braque would recall, scaling the cliffs of modernism. Their new style perplexed critics of the day who called it "cubism."

Picasso's 1911 painting, *The Glass of Absinthe*, is a masterpiece of analytic cubism. Here objects on a table top — a glass of absinthe, a fan, and a book — have been broken down and reformed in the painter's mind in a way that rebuts Renaissance perspective. As Picasso himself said to Christian Zervos, "I put all the things I like into my pictures. Too bad for the things, they just have to put up with it." The objects appear to be drawn from multiple viewpoints, resulting in a web of fragmented but interlocking shapes. Now the glass of absinthe is flattened, the fan turns in space, the book fits into the table like a puzzle piece. Shadows, planes, and volumes pass as freely through one another as the human mind allows memory, emotions, and time to transect and merge.

It wasn't easy being in the avant-garde. For example, in the November 1913 issue of the little magazine, *Les Soirées de Paris*, its new editor, Guillaume Apollinaire, published photographs of Picasso's previously unexhibited wall construc-

The Glass of Absinthe, 1911, was painted at the height of Picasso's analytic cubist period. Time, space, and perspective have been fragmented into a puzzle of interlocking forms and multiple points of view.

Picasso's *Bottle of Pernod and Glass*
was painted in the spring of 1912. Note
the clearly painted Pernod Fils label —
the premier absinthe manufacturer.

tions, *Guitar* and *Violin*. The next month, all but one of the fourteen magazine subscribers had canceled their subscriptions, evidently offended by the work. With admirable bravery, Picasso and his dealer Kahnweiler went ahead to issue the 1914 sculpture, *The Glass of Absinthe*, in an edition of six bronzes.

This piece was to be the only sculpture in the round that Picasso did between 1910 and 1926. In many ways it is the culmination of absinthe-inspired works. The wax model was cast in bronze and then topped with an absinthe spoon from a café and a bronze lump painted to look like sugar. The stem of the glass is integral, but the bowl has been distorted into swirling planes, a veritable storm in an absinthe glass. The polka dot pattern is a kind of theft of pointillism that gives the work a certain nostalgic humor.

It is easy to ascribe an anthropomorphic aspect to the glass and for one critic it conjured, "The top-heavy slanting hats and tight-fitting lace chokers of the ladies of those times." With a little imagination, one might see the sculpture as a distorted death's head, its tongue protruding with laughter, echoing a line from Apollinaire's book, *Alcools*: "Mon verre s'est brisé comme un éclat de rire." (My glass has shattered like a burst of laughter.)

In fact, Picasso expert Werner Spies said that Picasso was against such anthropomorphosis: "When I told him that one critic had seen the *Glass of Absinthe* as a face, wearing a spoon with sugar lump cap, he protested vehemently: 'I never intended that. What interested me was the relationship between the strainer and the form, the way they collided with each other.'"

Picasso frequented cafés such as the Lapin Agile and was surrounded by absinthe drinkers of all kinds. And absinthe was constantly being attacked in the press, by temperance groups, and in politics. Even puppet shows — which both Jarry and Picasso loved — featured plays which had absinthe as a villain. Charles Foley's one-act play *Absinthe* was first performed in 1913 at the Grand Guignol in Paris under the title *Le Vieux de la Rouquine*. It told the story of the decadent Baron de Lurcy, an absinthe addict. As the curtain rises on the Baron's household at morning, a housekeeper and valet are lamenting the Baron's destructive vice. "And when he awakes — it's terrible — he looks like a lost soul called back from another world — like one who dreams nightmares with his eyes open!"

When the Baron himself enters still dressed in his evening clothes stained with mud, he tells his

Picasso's *The Glass of Absinthe*, 1914, a painted bronze sculpture.

valet a vivid dream he had in which he murdered a red-haired harlot who snubbed him. As the valet dutifully undresses his master, he finds first a bloody scarf, then strands of long red hair twisted about one cufflink. It becomes obvious that his master has done more than dream the event. Confronted, the Baron is as surprised as his valet and innocently declares, "Even in a rage, even maddened by absinthe, I could never have done that!" In the midst of the revelation, the housekeeper interrupts to say that the police have arrived. The play is one-dimensional, dated, and unintentionally humorous, but at the time it must have impressed a great many people — certainly theater-going valets — that absinthe was a threat to morality and health.

Picasso's strange little sculpture would be the last great work of art inspired by absinthe. Like Jarry's play *Ubu roi*, Picasso's cubist translation of the absinthe glass showed that absurdity, ambiguity, and shattered convention could be recombined into art of a new order. But within six months of the sculpture's creation, absinthe itself would be banned.

142. *Compositae.*
13. *Artemisiae.*

LXX, 2.

587. *Artemisia Absinthium L.* **Wermuth.**

Artemisia absinthium, known as worm-wood or grande absinthe, is the essential ingredient in absinthe.

Chapter 7

The Origins of Ancient and Modern Absinthe

Long before it could be ordered in a café, absinthe was considered a vivifying elixir. When Madame de Coulanges, one of the leading ladies of the seventeenth-century French court, became ill, she was prescribed a preparation containing wormwood. When it calmed her stomach, she wrote to Madame de Sévigné, "My little absinthe is the remedy for all diseases."

Ancient absinthe was different from the liquor that Verlaine and Picasso imbibed, generally being wormwood leaves soaked in wine or spirits. References to it appear in the Bible, in Egyptian papyri, and early Syrian texts. Most likely the word *absinthe* derives from the Greek word *apsinthion*, which means "undrinkable" (presumably because of its bitter taste). Pythagoras recommended wormwood soaked in wine to aid labor in childbirth. Hippocrates prescribed it for jaundice, rheumatism, anemia, and menstrual pains. The Roman scholar Pliny the Elder called it *apsinthium* in the first century A.D. and noted that it was customary for the champion in chariot races to drink a cup of absinthe leaves soaked in wine to remind him that even glory has its bitter side. He also recommended it as an elixir of youth and as a cure for bad breath.

Wormwood, *Artemisia absinthium*, is a shrublike perennial belonging to the great family of Compositae, which are native to Europe and Asia. It is a long-lived, tenacious plant, two to four feet high with greyish-green leaves. The flowers have a greenish-yellow tint, have no pappus, and like the leaves, give off a strong aromatic odor and are bitter to the taste. The Compositae are a plant group consisting of 180 species which include tarragon (*Artemisia dracunculus*) as well as mugwort (*Artemisia vulgaris*).

Wormwood is supposed to have grown up along the path by which the serpent took exile from the Garden of Eden. Yet in some parts of Europe, wormwood is called "Girdle of St. John" and is believed to ward off evil spirits. Wormwood is mentioned in the Bible a dozen times. In the apocalyptic revelations of St. John we find, "And the third part of the waters became wormwood; and many men died of the waters, because they were made bitter." (By a strange coincidence, wormwood in Russian is *chernobyl*, the name of the Russian city which experienced a disastrous nuclear meltdown in 1986.)

Named for the goddess Diana, it appeared in an early translation of the *Herbarium* by Apuleius,

Wormwood, *Artemisia absinthium*, growing wild in the Val-de-Travers, Switzerland.

Hippocrates recommended it for jaundice and rheumatism.

the second-century Roman philosopher: "Of these worts that we name Artemisia, it is said that Diana did find them and delivered their powers and leechdom to Chiron the Centaur, who first from these Worts set forth a leechdom, and he named these worts for the name of Diana, Artemis, that is Artemisias."

Galen (131–201 A.D.) the greatest Greek physician after Hippocrates and founder of experimental physiology, was a strong advocate of absinthe's virtues, recommending absinthe in case of "debility or swooning" and suggesting that, "If one cannot cause vomiting and relaxation of the stomach with olive oil . . . one should give to drink an infusion of the heads of absinthia in melikraton, then wine." For fainting he counseled applying "fortifying cataplasms" over the stomach containing dates, wine, absinthe, and olive oil.

One of the earliest uses of wormwood was as a purge and vermifuge. In thirteenth-century France, essence of *assince* or *absince* was fed to dogs to cure flatulence, and by the fourteenth century *assenz* was recommended to aid human digestion. It was known as *absynce* in the fifteenth century, and Rabelais called it *absynthe* in 1546. The British herbalist John Gerard wrote in his 1597 book, *Herball,* that the plant, "Wormewood voideth away the wormes of the guts," hence the name. Not only good for ridding the intestines of worms, absinthe was recommended as a gastric tonic and heart stimulant.

Used externally, wormwood was a deterrent for vermin. *St Alban's Hawking Book* of 1486 described wormwood as a "medecyne for an hawke that hath mites. Take the Iuce of wormewode and put it ther that be and their shall dye." Thomas Middleton in *Anything For a Quiet Life* (1626) spoke of a man who burned wormwood "to kill the fleas i' the rushes." And Thomas Tusser, in his book, *July's Husbandry,* 1577, coined this couplet of good housekeeping: "Where chamber is swept, and wormwood is strown, no flea for his life dare abide to be knowne."

Wormwood also had a reputation as protection against the plague. During the seventeenth and eighteenth centuries in England, people sometimes slept with it in their pillows, hung it from rafter beams, and burned it to fumigate plague-infected houses.

Wormwood's reputation as a cure-all in England can be traced to herbalist Nicholas Culpepper. A 1780 edition of his herbal compendium calls wormwood "an herb of Mars" and attributes extraordinary powers to it based on the idea that "the herb is good for something, because God made nothing in vain." Culpepper notes further:

"Wormwood delights in Martial places, for about forges and iron works you may gather a car-load of it. It helps the evils Venus and the wanton boy produce. It remedies the evils choler[a] can inflict on the body of a man by sympathy. Wormwood being an herb of Mars, is a present remedy for the biting of rats and mice. Mushrooms are under the dominion of Saturn, if any have poisoned himself by eating them, Wormwood, an herb of Mars, cures him, because Mars is exalted in Capricorn. Suppose a man be bitten or stung by a hornet, a scorpion, Wormwood, and herb of Mars, gives you a present cure."

Over the centuries, however, wormwood drinks moved away from being just bitter medicine. Peter Morwyng, who published the *Treasures of Evonymous*, reported in 1559 that London apothecaries were no longer the sole distillers of wine for medicinal purposes. Independent distilleries were producing absinthe made from the dried leaves of wormwood steeped in equal parts of malmsey wine and "burning water thrice distilled." The "Purl" of Tudor England was compounded of ale or hot beer and wormwood, and although it was mainly popular with the working classes, Samuel Pepys reported in his famous diary that he had enjoyed several glasses of wormwood ale one night "in a little house . . . which doubtless was a bawdy house."

These dusty tales convey something of the mystique surrounding absinthe; one imagines a flask of it sitting beside the alchemist's crocodile and the mandrake root. Absinthe incorporated Olympian legends of debauch and rather down-home peasant notions.

Modern absinthe allegedly was invented in 1792 by an extraordinary French doctor called Pierre Ordinaire, who fled France's revolution to settle in Couvet, a small village in western Switzerland. On his periodic journeys by horseback, Dr. Ordinaire is said to have discovered the plant *Artemisia absinthium* growing wild in the hills of the Val-de-Travers region. Like most country doctors, he prepared his own remedies, and being acquainted with absinthe's use in ancient times, he began experimenting with it.

Dr. Ordinaire's recipe probably included the following herbs: wormwood, anise *(Pimpinella anisum)*, hyssop *(Hyssopus officinalis)*, dittany *(Dictamnus albus)*, sweet flag *(Acorus calamus)*,

Galen, the second century A.D. physician, promoted absinthe's virtues.

Seventeenth-century jar of "Absynthe."

87

Maison PERNOD Fils
1. - Vue d'ensemble des Etablissements

The Pernod factory on the Doubs River at Pontarlier, as it appeared at the turn of the century.

Melissa (a type of mint), and varying amounts of coriander, veronica, camomile, parsley, and even spinach. The 136 proof elixir produced in his sixteen liter still became popular as a cure-all in town and early on was nicknamed La Fée Verte. On his death, he supposedly left his secret recipe to two Henriod sisters from Couvet, who then left it to a visiting Frenchman, Major Dubied, whose son-in-law was named Pernod, and the rest is history.

Well, not exactly. Dr. Ordinaire did exist, did sell absinthe, and died in 1821, but as early as 1769 an advertisement for a "Bon Extrait d'Absinthe" had appeared in a Neuchâtel, Switzerland newspaper. It is now certain that the two Henriod sisters had been making absinthe long before Dr. Ordinaire's arrival in the Val-de-Travers. And, of course, the use of absinthe elixir and absinthiated wine goes back thousands of years. But to give him his due, Ordinaire most certainly was one of the first to promote La Fée Verte.

The next important figure in absinthe's history was Major Henri Dubied who bought a bottle of absinthe for indigestion from the Henriod sisters and found that in addition to providing a palpable high, it could cure chills, fevers, bronchial in-

Harvesting the wormwood crop near Pontarlier.

flammations, and low appetite. By 1797, Major Dubied had bought the Henriods' recipe and decided to market the product himself in the Val-de-Travers and in the neighboring mountains of the French Jura. That same year, his daughter Emilie married a Swiss fellow named Henri-Louis Pernod. Dubied, his son Marcellin, and Pernod set up a modest partnership in Couvet. The distillery measured eight-by-four meters, but as sales of absinthe increased, the plant was enlarged.

With the growing profits, in 1805, Henri-Louis Pernod opened a larger factory, Pernod Fils, twelve miles away across the border in Pontarlier, France — the first distillery of an anise-based liqueur in France. One of the main reasons for this move was to avoid paying high import taxes at the French border. Dubied and his eldest son split from Pernod and returned to Couvet, but his second son, Constant Dubied, passed Dubied Père et Fils (then rebased in Pontarlier) on to a cousin called Fritz Duval. And Dubied's daughter Cecile married a man called Rosselet who started a distillery in Pontarlier which eventually became known as Berthoud.

From here the family relations get more baroque. Pernod had two sons by two marriages.

Henri-Louis Pernod married Major Dubied's daughter and founded the house of Pernod.

Bags of dried wormwood were stored in the basement.

The eldest son, Edouard, remained in Couvet and in 1827 transferred the company to his own name. Eventually Edouard had a son also called Edouard, who started his own company in 1897.

The founder's younger son Louis (by second wife, Emilie Dubied) ran the Pernod Fils factory at Pontarlier, but pre-deceased his father. The distillery on the main street of Pontarlier was still tiny with two stills that produced only sixteen liters a day; but as business increased, Louis purchased 36,000 square meters of land on the banks of the Doubs River and built a factory with a daily production that exceeded 400 liters.

Like many businesses, past and present, Pernod benefited from war. From 1844–47, French troops fighting in Algeria were issued rations of absinthe as a fever preventative. Mixed with wine or water, absinthe was believed to kill microbes. Also, quite understandably, the high octane concoction must have alleviated the boredom of barracks life. It gave the troops a taste for anise, and when thousands of these soldiers returned to Paris, they brought the craving with them.

The custom quickly pervaded French society, aided by the Pernod brothers' business acumen and advertising. Pernod's twenty-six stills were soon producing 20,000 liters a day, and the factory was equipped with a shipping platform and spur linking to the railroad.

Louis Pernod died in 1850, and on December 6, 1853, founding father Henri-Louis followed at the age of seventy-seven. Louis's sons Louis-Alfred and Fritz, who had grown up playing hide-and-seek among the absinthe vats, took the helm of Pernod Fils under the tutelage of their mother Emilie and a meticulous Swiss engineer named Arthur Borel, who had designed the factory equipment and was the closest associate to three generations of Pernods.

Fritz Pernod died in 1880, and Louis-Alfred continued to run Pernod Fils, setting up regional depots with financing through a partnership in 1888 with Arthur Veil-Picard, an important banker from Besançon, France. The Pernod Fils brand name was retained, but the concern took

The distilling equipment at the Pernod plant was the most advanced of its day.

the name Veil-Picard & Compagnie, with Arthur and his brother Edmond as managers. When Louis-Alfred Pernod retired in 1894, Arthur Veil-Picard's three sons — Arthur, Edmond, and Léon — took over and successfully operated the firm so that by the turn of the century, their daily production of 30,000 liters was distributed to all parts of the world.

Absinthe put the little town of Pontarlier on the map. And the local voters were not ungrateful. In 1880, they elected Louis-Dionys Ordinaire, grandson of absinthe's first promoter, as a representative to the National Assembly. A few years later, they elected his son Maurice Ordinaire to represent them as a senator from the Doubs region. (An almost unbelievable coincidence is that Pernod Fils's current director of public relations is Jean-Marc Andrié, a direct descendant of the original Dr. Ordinaire!)

Out of 8,776 townspeople living in Pontarlier in 1906, some 500 worked for Pernod and the other distillers. Over 3,000 people in the Doubs Valley derived their livelihood from the cultivation and production of absinthe.

In addition to being the flagship industry of the town of Pontarlier, the company was a model of enlightened labor policy. As early as August 1873, Louis-Alfred and Fritz Pernod had introduced a profit-sharing plan which provided retirement pay for workers. At its own expense, the firm insured workers against accidents and gave them unemployment compensation, also paying half-wages to those who could not work because of illness. Bernard Lavergne noted in his book, *L'Evolution social* (1894), that "sympathy for the worker is traditional in this establishment."

The well-lighted and ventilated Pernod factory had nothing in common with the cramped industrial conditions described by Dickens or Zola. Machines did so much of the work that only 170 employees (almost half women) ran the twenty-six stills and twenty-two coloring tanks. Acoustical tubes transmitted orders. Elevators lifted stock from the basement. A machine could produce and

Maison PERNOD Fils
8. – Chantier d'expédition, empaquetage

Women wrapping absinthe bottles for packing.

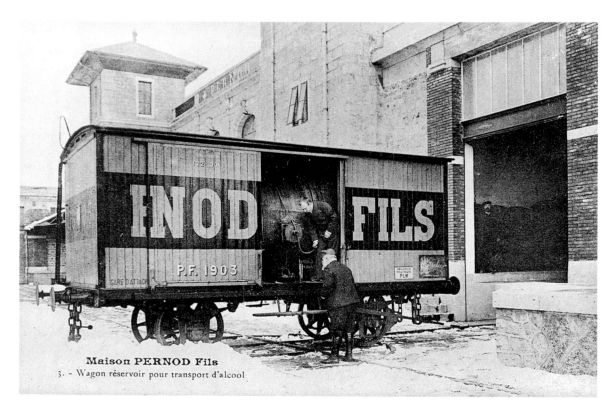

ENOD FILS

P.F. 1903

Maison PERNOD Fils
3. – Wagon réservoir pour transport d'alcool

A rail spur brought boxcars directly inside the Pernod plant for loading.

Garçon! Un Pierrot !!!

Pierrot Absinthe, a Pernod competitor. Some manufacturers, in an effort to achieve the proper shade of green in their product, had taken to adding indigo, turmeric, hyssop, nettles, aniline-green, or copper sulfate. Antimony chloride was sometimes added to assure the necessary "whitening" demanded by consumers, the toxic potential notwithstanding.

Below: Absinthe poster for H. Deniset, Jeune, one of twenty-two distilleries in Pontarlier.

After the fire, the plant was rebuilt with fire-proofing and the latest technical machinery. The loss to Pernod was over two million francs, but the clever Pernods were insured by six companies and collected almost 3,908,000 francs for damages. The new factory was finished just in time for the centennial of the company in 1905 — coincidentally, the same year that Jean Lanfray's murderous rampage set off the anti-absinthe movement in Switzerland.

Wormwood was grown in the region around Pontarlier and the greater Doubs Valley but also as far away as Besançon. It was also grown in the Jura, the Haute-Saône, the Haute-Marne, and outside of Paris. By 1908, there were 400 hectares of wormwood plants in the Doubs Valley. Planted in spring, it was harvested the following year in July before the stalks put out their flowers. A plant would live six years, but the maximum leaf production was in the second year. A farmer could expect 4,500 kilos of absinthe plant per hectare the second year but only 2,500 kilos in the sixth. The crop was picked by workers paid twenty centimes an hour, stacked to dry for a month, and then delivered to the distilleries.

The recipe for Pernod Fils and most of the other legitimate absinthes was six herbs: la grande absinthe for taste; la petite absinthe and hyssop for the green color; Melissa, a plant which is used, incidentally, in eau de cologne; fennel, the vege-

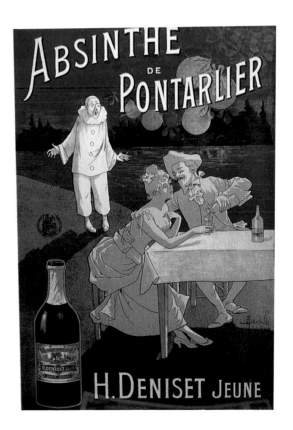

The Pernod factory was struck by lightning in 1901 and burned to the ground. Rebuilt within a year, it used the most modern technology.

The Old Absinthe House, New Orleans, circa 1910, photographed by Morgan Whitney.

table, which like Melissa, contributed to absinthe's taste and aroma; and finally anise (not to be confused with star anise or badiane). Pernod Fils used an eau-de-vie distilled from wine, unlike the producers of inferior absinthe who used an "industrial alcohol" produced from beets. The grandes and petites absinthe plants came from the region around Pontarlier, but the rest of the ingredients were shipped in: fennel from the Gard region of France and even from Italy, the anise from the Tarn region or from Andalusia, and eau-de-vie from Languedoc or Roussillon. The bottles were sent to Paris or to ports such as Marseilles and Le Havre — to be shipped as far away as Tahiti, Madagascar, Valparaiso, Montreal, Buenos Aires, Hanoi, and San Francisco.

Naturally, absinthe soon found its way to the Little Paris of North America, New Orleans. The drink, which was spelled *absynthe* in an 1837 New Orleans liquor advertisement, enjoyed a vogue under such brand names as Green Opal, Herbsaint, and Milky Way. (Today, one can still find a version of this made without wormwood and marketed under the name Herb Sainte.)

Of all the ancient buildings in New Orleans's famed French Quarter, none has been more glorified by drunks and postcard photographers alike than a square, plaster and brick structure at the corner of Bourbon and Bienville streets. "The Old Absinthe House" with its scarred cypress bar was visited by many famous people: Mark Twain, Oscar Wilde, Lafcadio Hearn, William Thackeray, Walt Whitman, Aaron Burr, and General P.G.T. Beauregard are just a few of the many who relaxed over a green absinthe in this shady retreat. Alexis, Grand Duke of all Russians, drank here, and the chairs once creaked under William Howard Taft's presidential bulk. The great O. Henry was just a struggling newspaperman named William Sidney Porter when he came to dream over an absinthe frappé.

The building was constructed in 1806 for the importing and commission firm of Juncadella & Font, two Catalans from Barcelona. In 1820, after Francisco Juncadella died and Pedro Font returned to his native Spain, the place continued as a commission house for the barter of foodstuffs, tobacco, clothing, and Spanish liquor. Relatives of the original owners turned it into an épicerie, then a bootshop. Finally, in 1846, the ground floor corner room became a saloon known as "Aleix's Coffee House," run by Jacinto Aleix and his brother, nephews of old Señora Juncadella.

The Old Absinthe House, New
Orleans, circa 1903.

The Old Absinthe House displays
the green marble fountains that once
dripped ice water into absinthe.

Edgar Allen Poe, 1848. Poe and his friend Henry Beck Hirst, a lawyer interested in international copyright records and ornithology, regularly visited the Philadelphia offices of publisher John Sartain, a well-known absinthe drinker. Here Poe and Hirst learned to drink what must have been a nearly fatal mixture of absinthe and brandy. After imbibing, Hirst, with his passion for birds, would morosely urge Poe to recite, once again, "The Raven." Poe's drinking brought an early death, but Baudelaire, who translated Poe into French, felt that alcohol was essential for Poe's writing, "a magic conveyance that transported him to the enchanted spaces of the unreal."

After sailing his fifty-foot yacht around the world, Jack London confessed in *John Barleycorn; or, Alcoholic Memoirs*, 1913: "So it was that I reached the Marquesas, the possessor of a real, man's size thirst. And in the Marquesas were several white men, a lot of sickly natives, much magnificent scenery, plenty of trade rum, an immense quantity of absinthe, but neither whiskey nor gin. . . . I had ever been plastic, and I accepted the absinthe. The trouble with the stuff was that I had to take such inordinate quantities in order to feel the slightest effect. . . . From the Marquesas I sailed with sufficient absinthe in ballast to last me to Tahiti." London's excesses led him to depression, financial ruin, and suicide at the age of forty.

James Gordon Bennett, Jr., founder of the *Paris Herald*, had a curious way of hiring staff. He used the "love me, love my dog technique." A job applicant would be made to wait in the office anteroom for an hour. Finally, a door would open and in would come not Bennett but Papillon, the publisher's black Pekinese. If the dog liked the applicant, he was as good as hired. If, however, Papillon followed his usual instincts and nipped at the visitor's trousers, Bennett would enter and dismiss the man. John Burke, a future editor of the *Paris Herald*, found his way around this obstacle. Before his interview, he consulted a dog fancier who told him that all canines love the odor of anisette. So on the appointed day, Burke downed a couple of glasses of absinthe and sprinkled some of the anise-flavored liqueur on his trousers. Papillon nearly leapt into his lap, and Burke was hired on the spot.

98

Absinthe House, New Orleans, painted
by Guy Pene du Bois.

In 1869, the Aleix brothers hired Cayetano
Ferrér, another Catalan, who had been a bar-
keeper at the French Opera House. In 1874, Cayetano himself leased the place and renamed it the
"Absinthe Room" because of the numerous re-
quests he had for the drink which he served in the
French manner. Stationed along the long cypress
bar were marble fountains with brass faucets
which slowly dripped cool water, drop by drop,
over the sugar cubes perched above the glasses.
Over the years, the place became known as "The
Old Absinthe House."

Absinthe was also drunk in San Francisco,
Chicago, and New York, which had a popular
restaurant called the Absinthe House. Up until
1912, many of the more exotic bars in New York
would serve an absinthe cocktail. One can imagine a piano player at one of these watering holes
singing this Victor Herbert melody with lyrics by
Glenn MacDonough:

It will free you first from burning thirst
That is born of a night of the bowl,
Like a sun 'twill rise through the inky skies
That so heavily hang o'er your souls.
At the first cool sip on your fevered lip
You determine to live through the day,
Life's again worth while as with a dawning smile
You imbibe your absinthe frappé.

But on July 13, 1907, *Harper's Weekly* noted,
"The growing consumption in America of absinthe, 'the green curse of France,' has attracted
the attention of the Department of Agriculture, and
an investigation has been ordered to determine to
what extent it is being manufactured in this country." Just five years later, on July 25, 1912, the
Department of Agriculture issued Food Inspection
Decision 147, which banned absinthe in America.

The Green Fairy as deathly temptress,
engraving by Apoux.

Chapter 8

The Medical Case against Absinthe

For years doctors had been gathering testimony against absinthe to charge that it interfered with normal development of the fetus, caused illness in the digestive organs and central nervous system, encouraged tuberculosis, abetted criminality, and led to insanity.

The most important studies were conducted by Dr. Valentin Magnan (1835–1916), the illustrious physician at the asylum of Sainte-Anne in Paris. A respected authority on alcoholic insanity, he spent his life investigating absinthe and leading the fight for its prohibition. In 1864, as part of a general study on madness, Magnan began experimenting with alcohol and absinthe on guinea pigs, cats, rabbits, birds, and dogs.

One of Magnan's early experiments was described in an 1869 issue of *The Lancet*. A guinea pig was placed under a glass case with a saucer of wormwood oil by its side. Another guinea pig was similarly imprisoned in a glass case with a saucer containing pure alcohol. A cat and a rabbit were respectively encased along with saucers full of wormwood oil. Magnan observed that the three animals which inhaled the vapors of wormwood became excited and then had epileptiform convulsions while the guinea pig that breathed the alcoholic fumes merely became drunk.

Magnan then forced dogs to ingest large quantities of alcohol, driving the animals to the point of hallucination and death. He concluded that alcohol did not cause epileptic or epileptiform convulsions in animals. However, when the animals were given small doses of absinthe absorbed through the stomach, Magnan found this provoked an *état vertigineux* resembling the *petit mal* form of epilepsy. Large doses of absinthe produced full-blown epileptic attacks.

Magnan's studies led him to conclude that absinthe produced reactions in human beings distinct from alcoholic delirium tremens. In 1874, Magnan studied 250 acute cases of alcoholism and concluded that while normal alcoholics suffered from delirium tremens, absinthists were prone to epileptic convulsions called "absinthe epilepsy" caused by lesions on the brain tissue. Magnan concentrated his study on absinthe's prime ingredient, wormwood, whose derivative essence is thujone. The results suggested that thujone affected the motor center of the cerebrum and the paracerebellar nuclei, producing convulsions and hallucinations of sight and hearing. Chronic users of absinthe, Magnan declared, were subject to a kind of automatism and amnesia, violence, and epileptic seizures.

Dr. Valentin Magnan devoted his life to studying the effects of absinthe and alcohol.

The Absinthe Demon by Jacques Sourian, 1910.

"In absinthism, the hallucinating delirium is most active, most terrifying, sometimes provoking reactions of an extremely violent and dangerous nature. Another more grave syndrome accompanies this: all of a sudden the absinthist cries out, pales, loses consciousness and falls; the features contract, the jaws clench, the pupils dilate, the eyes roll up, the limbs stiffen, a jet of urine escapes, gas and waste material are brusquely expulsed. In just a few seconds the face becomes contorted, the limbs twitch, the eyes are strongly convulsed, the jaws gnash and the tongue projected between the teeth is badly gnawed; a bloody saliva covers the lips, the face grows red, becomes purplish, swollen, the eyes are bulging, tearful, the respiration is loud, then the movements cease, the whole body relaxes, the sphincter releases, the evacuations soil the sick man. Suddenly he lifts his head and casts his eyes around him with a look of bewilderment. Coming to himself after awhile, he doesn't remember one thing that happened. This is an epileptic attack. Other times, the manifesta-tions are less noisy: the individual pales, some small twitches appear at the corner of his mouth and for an instant he is a stranger, oblivious to all that passes around him: he experiences giddiness."

Magnan was an advanced practitioner in his field of drugs and alcohol; the itching symptoms of cocaine addiction, for example, are named "Magnan's Sign" after his research. And he was one of the first to treat alcoholics as mentally ill. The fact that he looked for psychological causes of the disease at a time when Freud was still a young medical student is admirable. But, as Patricia E. Prestwich has written, "his effectiveness was limited by his preoccupation with the so-called 'degeneration' of the French race and by his unbending conviction that alcohol was the prime cause of most mental disorders."

Magnan's interpretations of alcoholism and particularly absinthism were oversimplified and alarmist. From clinical observation he concluded that absinthe caused medical and psychological troubles not associated with the high consumption

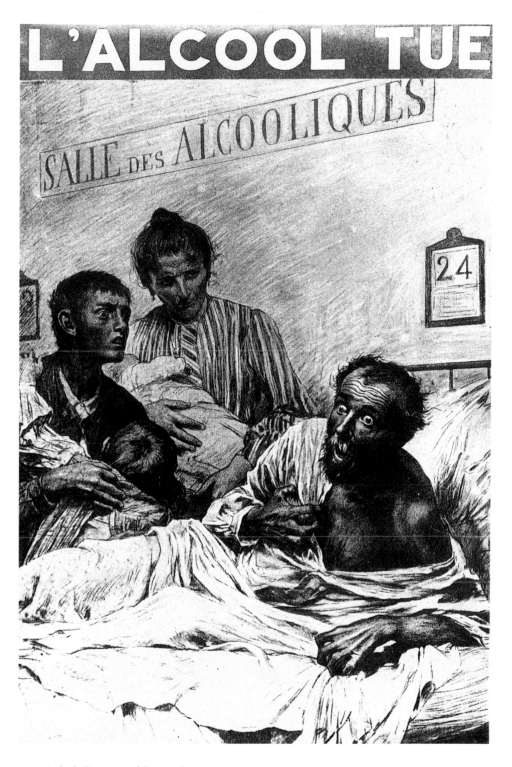

An anti-alcoholic poster of the age. During the 1880s, an absinthe was known in
slang as "une correspondance," which
was short for "une correspondance pour
Charenton" (a ticket to Charenton, the
insane asylum on the outskirts of Paris).

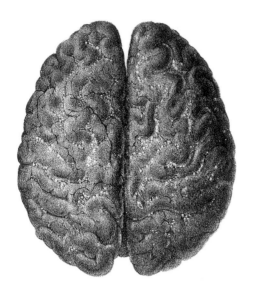

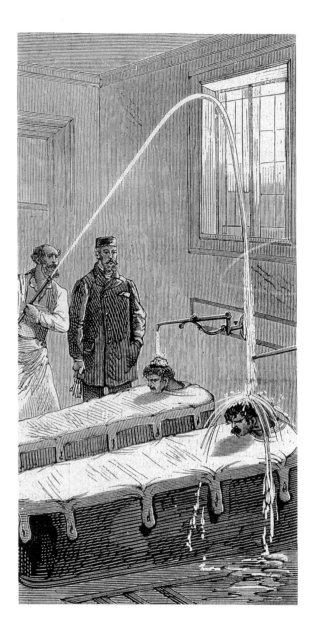

Brain of an alcoholic with meningitis.

Right: Hydrotherapy was the typical way of treating insanity or alcohol addiction in nineteenth-century asylums. Patients would be immersed for up to five hours a day.

of alcohol. Today we know that many of these diseases have more diverse origins than either alcohol or absinthe. Magnan also argued that absinthe's deleterious effects were not only rapid and irreversible, but hereditary — that they could be passed down to offspring. While the child of an alcoholic might inherit a tendency to alcoholism and madness, the child of an *absinthiste*, Magnan asserted, would be born with a predisposition to insanity and serious nervous problems. "Absinthe," wrote Prestwich, "was quickly associated with the most frightening and least understood of diseases, mental illness."

Magnan's early research was supported by other doctors conducting laboratory experiments in the toxicity of essences in the 1880s and 1890s. Further studies on dogs and guinea pigs purported to show that essence of wormwood followed by alcohol was far more potent than either element administered separately.

Distillation of wormwood oil (*oleum absinthii*) was apparently known as early as the sixteenth century, but the first chemical investigation of the oil was not undertaken until 1845. The principal fraction of the rectified oil, today known as thujone, was determined to be an isomer of camphor,

An anti-absinthe cartoon from the anti-alcoholic league's newspaper, *L'Étoile bleue*.

"Ah! Evil absinthe! It's because I believed in you that I'm reduced to this!" says an addict caricatured in *L'Étoile bleue*.

$C_{10}H_{16}O$. Thujone is unquestionably a powerful drug on its own when taken in substantial amounts. Though wormwood oil was prescribed by pharmacists from France to America for certain illnesses such as fevers, as early as 1872, the British medical journal, *The Lancet*, stated that its principal effects were in fact epileptiform attacks. Even in France, the same year, a law was passed so that pharmacists could not sell wormwood oil without prescription from a medical doctor.

Yet there were still doubts as to which ingredient in absinthe was the culprit. Dr. J.A. Laborde who presented a paper on essences in absinthe to the French Academy of Medicine on October 1, 1889 emphasized that the "accidents characteristic of the liqueur absinthe, currently and classically documented and known as Absintheisme [*sic*], should also, and with good reason, be called Anisisme."

Dr. Laborde says Magnan was mistaken in placing the blame completely on essence of wormwood because he did not make a thorough comparative study of the other essences in the drink. Indeed, tests conducted in 1957 at the Institute of Pharmacology at Bâle University revealed that essence of anise, anethol, combined with alcohol made animals more excited and irritated than if the animals ingested the anethol and alcohol separately.

In 1889, two French scientists, M. Cadéac and A. Meunier, conducted experiments on themselves — "because man alone is able to give an account of the phenomenon subjectively, such as loss of memory, of the will, and other intellectual problems." And they did not just study wormwood and thujone. Investigating all the ingredients in absinthe, they found that other herbs had powerful, damaging qualities. Their studies showed that hyssop, for example, was "une essence dangereuse, une essence convulsivante et epileptisante." They found that anise caused drowsiness and muscle resolution. An average dose produced "stupification," trembling, vision troubles, and headaches. Melissa proved to be a "soporific," while oregano induced vertigo, trembling, and obscured memory. In short, they were able to divide the ingredients into two camps: hyssop, wormwood, and fennel were "epileptisants" while anise, angelica, oregano, Melissa, and mint were "stupefiants."

"They want to suppress alcoholism! Bah! I'll always have my rifle at the ready!" Lithograph by Stop.

Countless testimony by doctors purported that absinthe drinkers were prone to a curious anguish and violence. Absinthe was also blamed for tuberculosis: Dr. Emile Lancereaux wrote in 1903 that nutrition declines with habitual drinking of apéritifs due to nausea and loss of appetite, and that progressive weight loss led to illness, tuberculosis,

Cusenier promoted absinthe with this jolly fellow and the line: "C'est ma santé" (It is healthy).

and finally death. "Observation shows that malnutrition is faster in drinkers of bitters and apéritifs than with regular drinkers of alcohol, and tuberculosis comes quicker and more frequently." And Dr. Louis Landouzy coined the phrase, "Alcohol makes the bed for tuberculosis." The disease preys on the malnutritioned — which most alcoholics are — but no clinical results showed that absinthe caused more malnutrition or tuberculosis than any other alcoholic drink.

We now know that alcohol itself is an addictive substance. But was absinthe more addictive than other alcoholic beverages? Probably not. The tendency of the absinthe drinker was to start drink-

An absinthe poster by Bensa-Dupont
circa 1900.

ing it with water and gradually to take it almost
straight, which, of course, makes the alcohol
intake higher. Yet even a full bottle of absinthe
should be condemned more for its high alcohol
content than its thujone content. (See Appendix.)

But not all the physicians were against absinthe.
A number of them highly endorsed it if taken in

Absinthe Terminus.

moderation. For example, in 1904, several pro-absinthe doctors published a pamphlet, *Opinions Scientifiques sur l'Absinthe*, that supported the medicinal aspects of the drink. Some recommended it for gout, others for dropsy. Dr. Antoine Bossu prescribed it as a general stimulant, vermifuge, and febrifuge.

Dr. Albert Ragnard even felt that it stimulated the brain for intellectual activity: "les facultés intellectuelles peuvent être portées à leur maximum d'intensité." Another physician, Dr. Pagès from the Seine region, wrote that on hot days, "Absinthe allows one to absorb, without danger of indigestion and general depression, great quan-

Absinthe Parisienne.

tities of water." He recommended it for bakers, glassblowers, and workers laboring under the hot sun, noting that the mechanics and stokers on the railroad used it heavily diluted during the hot summer of 1898.

Dr. Charles Borne, senator from the Doubs and former president of the Hygiene Commission in the Chamber of Deputies, enthused over absinthe as a refreshing drink in torrid climates and gave it credit for the French success in colonizing Africa. "Look at the colonies, the Italians, who by the use of their *gelati* (ice cream) destroy the stomach, catch fevers and other intestinal maladies, which the French colonials victoriously resist in this climate thanks to absinthe." Doctor Borne even quoted a colonial authority: "The venerable bishop of Madagascar, Mgr. Cazet, likes to repeat that he couldn't have survived such a murderous climate for forty-five years if he hadn't had the help of absinthe and he cites one of his missionaries, now eighty-six years old, who swears by the green liqueur for saving him in all his activities. This drinker is not just a holy priest, but also a savant and explorer: R.P. Roblet, the esteemed author of the map of Madagascar. . . .

"Our ancestors, who conquered Algeria, did so with the ingenious resource of 'absinthe soup' which guarded them against pernicious fevers." But, Dr. Borne lamented, when the anti-alcoholic league convinced the army to eliminate rations of absinthe to troops serving in Madagascar, the result was disastrous. "Anyone possessing absinthe was severely punished and each one was obliged to drink, *sans correctif*, the pestilent waters along the route. The result? 6,000 cadavers scattered on the road from Majunga to Tananarive!"

But the most extraordinary report came from a scientist named Van Helmont whose logic would have amused Alfred Jarry himself. Disturbed that all the absinthe experiments on animals had been conducted by injecting these animals with large doses of absinthe, Van Helmont decided to put the vote to the animals themselves. He gathered four five-liter water tanks, labeled A, B, C, and D. He then proceeded as follows:

"Tank A was filled with three liters of distilled water, chemically pure, boiled and allowed to cool at air temperature; the bottom of the tank was filled with gravel sterilized at 130 degrees Celsius; in the tank were placed two freshwater fish, two saltwater fish, and a frog; a little wooden ladder (sterilized at the same time as the gravel) would permit the frog to leave his tank.

"Tank B was filled with three liters of seawater (gathered at Trouville, at the end of the jetty-promenade) and lined with gravel and a ladder as before, and in this tank were put two freshwater fish and a frog.

"Tank C was filled with three liters of spring water (from Dhuys), gravel and a ladder, and in it were placed two saltwater fish and a frog.

"Tank D was filled with three liters of spring water (Dhuys) and one centiliter of sixty degree commercial absinthe. No special brand name. Only a frog was placed in this tank with a ladder and the gravel.

"This is what resulted:

"1) The four fish in Tank A died; the frog left to lodge himself in Tank D.

"2) The two fish in Tank B died; this frog also went to Tank D.

"3) The two fish in Tank C died; the third frog joined his colleagues in Tank D."

Van Helmont concluded:

"1) Distilled water, chemically pure and boiled, is a poison since the four fish plunged in it died quickly; the frog did not give his last salute because he climbed the ladder in a lively manner and took refuge in Tank D.

"2) Sea water is a poison, since the two fish placed in it died quickly; the frog left hastily.

"3) Spring water is a poison, since the two fish put in it also died.

"4) Spring water with a small quantity of absinthe spirits is a very clean environment because the four frogs took refuge there and seemed to stay there with pleasure."

This experiment was not intended as a joke.

Though newspapers backed the anti-absinthe campaign, not all readers did. Lithograph by H.G. Ibels, the cover of an 1892 theater program.

Chapter 9
Absinthe and Politics

After the Lanfray murder in 1905 and the subsequent ban on absinthe in Switzerland, anti-alcoholic sentiment rapidly gained momentum in France, supported by a coalition of the left and right wings. Henri Robert, leading criminal barrister at the French bar, was quoted in the London *Times* (August 12, 1907): "Alcoholism is the chief cause of the increase in criminality. Absinthe is the enemy."

In 1906, Edouard Drumont, author of *La France juive* (1886) and the premier anti-Semitic intellectual of the day, introduced a racist note into absinthe's strange history. In his newspaper, *La Libre Parole*, Drumont claimed that absinthe was a nefarious "tool of the Jews," referring no doubt to the fact that Arthur and Edmond Veil-Picard, who had just purchased a controlling interest in the Pernod Fils Company, were half-Jewish. This would seem an insignificant if unpleasant footnote, were it not for the fact that France had just been through the Dreyfus Affair.

In 1894, Captain Dreyfus was accused of passing information to the Germans and was summarily condemned to life imprisonment on Devil's Island. France was going through a vogue of spy-phobia, so this was nothing new except that Dreyfus was highly placed on the army's general staff. The French army was strict — lesser crimes such as desertion were often treated with death sentences — and the first press accounts merely complained that the military had not been been tough enough on a spy. (Actually, early newspaper reports did not even mention the fact that the accused officer was a Jew.)

It took almost three years for the facts of the Dreyfus Affair to become public. Even when it was obvious that Dreyfus had been framed, the French military was unwilling to admit they had made an error. It was at this point that novelist Emile Zola wrote his famous "J'accuse" in the newspaper, *L'Aurore* — an open letter calling for justice from the French president. The result was explosive. Zola himself was brought to trial; there were riots in the street; Major Henry, who had forged documents "proving" Dreyfus's guilt, committed suicide. As facts about the frame-up were revealed, the case divided France into two camps. People were either for Dreyfus, a *Dreyfusard*, or against him (and anything else they thought Dreyfus or Jews in general represented). For example, it drove Degas to fire his favorite model because she was a Protestant "and all Protestants are for Dreyfus." But Monet, who had broken with Emile Zola after he criticized one of Monet's paintings in the Salon

Right: Edouard Drumont, framed by his anti-Semitic newspaper, *La Libre Parole*, which called absinthe "a tool of the Jews." This headline condemns the "traitor" Captain Dreyfus, who was falsely convicted for spying.

Below: The Dreyfus Affair inspired a brand called Absinthe Anti-Jew, with a xenophobic sub-legend, "France for the French."

Bottom: This Marseilles absinthe label appeared in 1900, six years after a knife-wielding anarchist assassinated President Sadi Carnot.

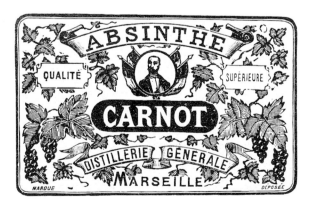

of 1896, suddenly wrote to congratulate the author's courageous stance with "Bravo! et Bravo encore!" Eventually, Dreyfus was released and the real villain, Commandant Esterhazy, was punished, but it is extraordinary how this affair divided a nation.

In 1898, absinthe and anti-Semitism met in a bizarre fashion — over an absinthe bottle. A lesser known manufacturer at Montbeliard (in the Doubs Valley) labeled his bottles "Absinthe Anti-Juive" (Anti-Jewish) with the sub-legend "France aux Français" (France for the French). Its success is undocumented, but the story indicates the factionalism and insecurity France suffered at the time.

Another absinthe label of 1900 from a Marseilles distiller respectfully depicted the late-President Sadi Carnot, who had been stabbed to death in 1894 by an Italian anarchist. France's government was in such disarray that when Emile Loubet became president of the republic in 1899, few imagined that he would be the first to serve out his full term — of his six predecessors, four had resigned, one had been murdered (Carnot), and the last incumbent, Felix Faure, had died in his mistress's arms — though there were rumors he had been poisoned by the Dreyfusards. Five days after Emile Loubet took office, there was an attempted coup d'état. Still later, Loubet had his top hat smashed with a cane by a drunken nobleman at the race-track — the man was an anti-Dreyfusard. The next few years were a time of anarchism, socialism, strikes, and concern over the military might of Germany.

But in the evenings at l'heure verte, the cafés of Paris and Marseilles were filled with men forgetting their cares over tall glasses of cloudy green liquid. Absinthe had become more than just a beverage or fad; it was a national pastime for bourgeois and worker alike. Until the late 1870s, absinthe had been relatively expensive and its consumption restricted to the middle class and comfortable Bohemians. When disease (phylloxera) attacked France's vineyards in the 1880s, the resultant shortage of wine led to increased consumption of absinthe. Absinthe producers began catering to a working-class market. Even when the wine crisis ended, absinthe's working-class drinkers remained faithful, and by 1894, a writer in *Le Temps* observed, "from the Nord to the Midi, from the Alps to the ocean, absinthe is queen."

In 1874, France consumed 700,000 liters of absinthe, but by 1910, the figure had risen to an astounding 36,000,000 liters of absinthe a year. More than just a threat to the wine business or sobriety, absinthe was viewed as a cause of France's unhealthy national condition.

An article in the socialist paper, *L'Humanité*, declared that absinthe was the primary stumbling block of the working classes in their struggle to attain dignity. "The worker who spends his salary on apéritifs isn't just a bad father, a bad worker, but also a detestable comrade who lets down the entire working class," said one socialist deputy.

Alcohol consumption and alcoholism continued to rise at an alarming rate, to the point where, in 1900, France was the largest consumer of alcohol in the world, the average per capita intake being eighteen liters a year (including wine, beer, cider, and other alcohols). The trend seemed to be away from wine toward the stronger drinks.

As the phylloxera crisis made traditional wine alcohol scarce, some absinthe manufacturers employed cheaper industrial alcohol made from beets or grain. A glass of absinthe could be sold for ten centimes — less than a glass of wine in some cases. Although there were 1500 different apéritifs in France, absinthe rapidly became the most popular,

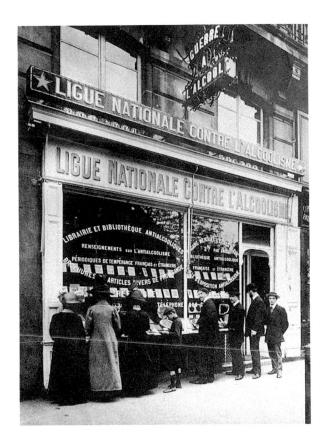

Temperance league office in Paris, 1900.

accounting for 90 percent (by volume) of the apéritif consumption.

But statistics can be deceptive. One might get the impression absinthe was taking over the country. Actually, absinthe never made up more than 3 percent of the alcohol drunk in France, while wine accounted for 72 percent (the remaining 25 percent being split among beer, eau-de-vie, and other drinks). And of the 2.3 million hectoliters of pure alcohol produced in France every year, only one-tenth went into the production of absinthe.

Consumption of absinthe increased steadily. For manufacturers, this meant fifteen million francs in annual revenues, and by 1914, surtaxes on absinthe put over fifty million francs in the national treasury — 1 percent of the annual budget.

The temperance movement in France began in 1872 with the formation of the *Société française contre l'abus des boissons alcooliques*. Soon it counted the support of eminent doctors, scientists, hygienists, politicians, and social reformers of all

Top: Pierre Henri Schmidt, deputy of the Vosges region, battled incessantly to ban absinthe.

Above: Dr. Philippe Grenier was elected to represent Pontarlier, despite the fact that as a Muslim, he opposed the consumption of alcohol.

persuasions, including early socialists. In 1907, there were 1,250 *sections anti-alcooliques* comprising 52,471 members who had renounced alcohol and were ready to make the rest of the nation quit, too. But for all their energy and propaganda, the temperance movement remained disorganized and plagued by infighting and financial problems.

The years 1906 and 1907 were a key period in the absinthe battle. After Switzerland voted to ban absinthe, the fervor spread to France. That year, the French *Ligue National Contre L'Alcoolisme* gathered 400,000 signatures on a petition which declared: "Absinthe makes one crazy and criminal, provokes epilepsy and tuberculosis, and has killed thousands of French people. It makes a ferocious beast of man, a martyr of woman, and a degenerate of the infant, it disorganizes and ruins the family and menaces the future of the country."

In the National Assembly, the anti-alcoholic movement tended to cross party lines. Absinthe's most notable opponent was Henri Schmidt, an apothecary who served as deputy from the Vosges (a region near the German border). Schmidt, a bombastic orator in the Chamber of Deputies, would proclaim: "We're not attacking the hour of the apéritif, this agreeable moment of detente. We are attacking the erosion of the national defense. The abolition of absinthe and the national defense are the same. What is necessary is trench warfare against absinthism!" Schmidt also told the assembly that by his calculations, absinthe was 246 times more likely to cause insanity than wine and was three times more guilty than other distilled alcohols. Schmidt argued, "The real characteristic of absinthe is that it leads straight to the madhouse or the courthouse. It is truly 'madness in a bottle' and no habitual drinker can claim that he will not become a criminal."

The pro-absinthe faction was less well organized at first and had fewer friends in government, but it seemed to have the right friends — except in one bizarre instance. Traditionally, deputies from the Doubs region fought for the honor of the Green Fairy; but when Louis-Dionys Ordinaire, a descendant of the original promoter of absinthe, Dr. Ordinaire, died in 1896, leaving his seat in the National Assembly vacant, the local voters of Pontarlier elected a peculiar native son, Dr. Philippe Grenier.

Though born to a strict Catholic family, Grenier had spent time in Algeria and returned as a convert to Islam, a religion which forbids alcohol of any kind. Grenier must have cut a strange figure when he arrived in Paris dressed in a turban and burnous, while his colleagues wore cutaways and top hats. The journals of the day caricatured him, while a few popular songs sprang up about the first Muslim to sit in Parliament. Dr. Grenier hoped to convince his constituents to turn away from absinthe production and instead to raise raspberries for syrup and jam. Within seventeen months, the people of Pontarlier took advantage of a new election to get a less conspicuous candidate.

In 1906, Pontarlier elected its most ardent absinthe supporter, Adolphe Girod, a man famous for his well-spoken, even lofty remarks. He never tired of standing in front of the chamber and elegantly mocking the temperance slogan that "absinthe makes a ferocious beast of man," by asking if the chamber found him, a man who enjoyed a daily ration of absinthe, anything like a mad dog.

Outside of parliament, Pontarlier had another strong ally in its *procureur pour la république* (district attorney), Edmond Couleru, who would have seemed an unlikely supporter of absinthe. A God-fearing Protestant who carried his own prayerbook to church, Couleru had an austere outlook on life and its excesses. But he made a strong defense for the Green Fairy when, in 1908, he published a 246-page book with the unusually long title: *Au pays de l'Absinthe — Y est-on plus criminel qu'ailleurs ou moins sain de corps et d'esprit? — Un peu de statisque, s.v.p.* (In the Land of Absinthe: Is one more criminal here than elsewhere or less sane in body or spirit? Some statistics, please).

True to his book title, Couleru served up statistics, graphs, and polemics. In one chapter he compared the criminal offense statistics vis-à-vis absinthe consumption in Pontarlier and Saint-Dié. Couleru chose Saint-Dié because it resembled Pontarlier in topography, climate, ethology, and economy. But it also happened that Saint-Dié was in the Vosges, the region represented by the rabidly anti-absinthe apothecary, Henri Schmidt. And Pontarlier triumphed in comparison. Couleru completed his study with pictures of healthy, happy peasants tending verdant fields of absinthe. The book argued that statistically the inhabitants were healthier than the average Frenchman, but then, as one deputy remarked, "Statistics is a whore who will accompany anyone."

Schmidt was undaunted. He, too, could use statistics. In his 1907 report proposing a law to ban the fabrication and sale of absinthe, Deputy Schmidt claimed that the number of insane had

Top: Adolphe Girod, deputy from Pontarlier, was the absinthe industry's most dedicated supporter, even after the ban.

Above: Dr. Pierre Legrain said, "The juice of absinthe is toxic the same way that the juice of belladonna is."

117

Dr. Jacques Roubinovitch declared in 1907: "When I go to the *prison de la Santé*, my eye is immediately drawn to a blackboard on which is written in crayon a number which hardly ever varies. This morning it was 1025. That's the total number of prisoners. Do you know how many among these unfortunates owe their insanity or their crimes to absinthe and similar apéritifs? About 600, and that's more than 60 percent."

grown in France over the last thirty years. "In 1871 there were 49,589 lunatics and by 1901 there were 100,291. What role did alcohol and particularly absinthe play in this growth?"

The temperance bloc began parading eminent physicians through the Chamber of Deputies to sully absinthe's reputation. Dr. Emile Lancereaux testified that men — especially working-class men — who drank "essences" became more tubercular. The minister of justice blamed rising crime and juvenile delinquency on alcohol and absinthe in particular. Absinthe was alleged to be a cause of working-class agitation, no doubt because workers were switching from "traditional" wine to absinthe. The drop in France's birthrate, the increase in suicides, and the high number of conscripts deemed unfit for military service also "proved" the theory that absinthe caused hereditary damage. Scientific publications and temperance propaganda tracts regularly printed pictures of the malformed and imbecilic offspring of absinthe drinkers. When doctors produced these photographs at parliamentary hearings, their effect was profound: it seemed to signify the degeneration of the whole French race. Absinthe, as one parliamentary critic put it, "was the maximum of poison, condensed, refined, perfumed, irresistible."

Each time an anti-absinthe bill was brought to the floor, lack of consensus gave absinthe another temporary reprieve. Schmidt worked tirelessly, arguing with figures showing that absinthe drinking was increasing thoughout the country. (Actually, official statistics from the French Ministry of Finance showed that while absinthe consumption had increased yearly until 1900, it had dropped somewhat by the time of the debates.)

Edmond Couleru, author of *Au Pays de l'Absinthe*, addressed the chamber and the senate on behalf of the industry at Pontarlier. There are two kinds of absinthe, he claimed, deluxe and ordinary. There is good absinthe and bad absinthe. Those bottled with a reputable label, those without. Those made from high-quality alcohol, those made with lower quality and with artificial essences manufactured by the chemical industry. Unfortunately, a member of the government's commission on alcoholism testified that the "better" absinthes were really worse for a person than the "lesser" quality because they delivered the essence of wormwood with a higher level of alcohol.

The torch-lit Place Clichy during the 1907 electrician's strike. The only sensible thing to do was to retire to a café and have an "abs," as regular drinkers called absinthe.

Absinthe Berthelot poster.

Le Péril Vert or Green Peril, an anti-
absinthe postcard.

"Absinthe Rend Fou" (Absinthe Makes
You Crazy) says this postcard.

The only medical doctor in the senate to support absinthe was Charles Borne, senator from the Doubs, who said, "I maintained and I affirm that absinthe obtained by distillation doesn't present the dangers of all these green poisons that one so justly accuses. True, one makes and sells absinthe at three sous (fifteen centimes). . . . This poison, we denounce it, but absinthe made by distillation, which còsts five and a half francs a liter and is sold to the consumer at fifty, sixty, and sixty-five centimes a glass, *this* absinthe will not be drunk by everybody." If the cheaper brands were banned, he implied, the working classes would stop drinking it.

Borne and the "pure liquor people" became the subject of mockery in the press. After Senator Borne from Pontarlier delivered his impassioned plea to the senate, Dr. Jacquet, who served on the government commission, wrote about the senator:

"He describes absinthe as composed of 'diuretics, tonics, stimulants, vermifuges, febrifuges, *lénitifs* — a perfumed and aromatic synergy, an assembly of plant extracts extremely favorable to the public health. A magnificent, a precious liquor,' he calls it in lyric flight. 'It contains only the finest alcohol, ethyl alcohol, rectified, pure. Then there are the perfumes and aromas — subtle, sublimated, ethereal, quintessential. We swim in full ether, in the broad azure. Where is the poison?' cries the honorable Senator. One is ashamed to curse such immaterial ambrosia. Then he goes on to contrast adulterated absinthes. He precipitates us from the seventh heaven to the ninth circle of the Inferno, 'wastes, gross residues, phlegms, heavy rheums.'"

In 1907, the president of the conseil, Georges Clemenceau, championed by the anti-alcoholic group in parliament, prescribed an inquest into the illnesses of inmates in the insane asylums. The report presented was surprisingly in absinthe's favor: Out of 71,547 individuals, 9,944 (one-seventh) were alcoholics. Of this group, only 1,537 were classified as absinthe drinkers, or about one-fortieth of the total. The report also had a breakdown of which region produced the most mentally disturbed alcoholics. Lunatics admitted from the Morbihan region showed alcoholism as high as 36 percent, but the average annual per capita consumption of absinthe was established at less than one-fifth of a liter. Similarly, high alcoholism and low absinthe consumption were reported in the Mayenne and Somme departments. In contrast, the big absinthe-consuming departments such as les Bouches-du-Rhône and le Var only recorded 12.2 percent and 4 percent respectively in regard to madmen who drank alcohol of any kind.

The government report also indicated that the regions that consumed the most alcohol were not necessarily those that consumed the most absinthe.

Edmond Couleru, *procureur de la république* for Pontarlier, proudly commented, "In the region of Pontarlier, center of the absinthe industry, the pathological phenomenon and disorders attributed to this drink are less prevalent than in the departments where one consumes great quantities of alcohol in other forms." The director of the asylum at Doubs reported that "of 190 hospitalized men, only forty-two were alcoholic and of these not one could be called an absinthe drinker."

One strike against Couleru's theories was that Pontarlier had the highest death rate in France. But much of this was attributed to unhealthy mountain air and violence caused by military troops stationed nearby. And as for crime, Couleru showed that while absinthe consumption was up in Pontarlier, criminal offences were down. Nonetheless, the rest of France was proving there was a correlation between alcoholism and crime.

Before 1900, an anti-absinthe crusade emerged. The anti-alcoholic league, the Academy of Medicine, the press, and even the unions began applying pressure to the government and the general public. The Academy of Medicine fired an opening salvo on March 10, 1903, when it passed a resolution calling for the ban on all apéritifs made from natural or artificial essences.

The anti-alcoholic league published a monthly revue called *L'Étoile bleue* (16,000 copies) which reported in 1907: "Almost all the papers fire up the civil and patriotic zeal of their readers to make them combat the most formidable of modern scourges." The temperance movement had the support of *Le Petit Parisien*, *L'Intransigeant*, *Le Petit Journal*, *L'Aurore*, *L'Action*, and above all, the left wing daily, *Le Matin*. (On the other hand, certain newspapers like *Le Siècle* defended the commerce of liquor under the banner of liberty.)

By 1897, anti-alcoholic instruction had become obligatory in schools all over France. Even dictation had an anti-absinthe theme. The league started 2,000 anti-alcoholic sections in schools, instructing teachers to tell children not to drink any alcohol until the age of twenty — if at all. Students founded their own organizations and became apostles of the cause. Poems such as the following appeared:

"Notre Dame de L'Oubli" (Our Lady of Oblivion) is the spirit of absinthe, according to this postcard.

I am the Green Fairy
My robe is the color of despair
I have nothing in common with the fairies of
the past
What I need is blood, red and hot, the palpitat-
ing flesh of my victims
Alone, I will kill France, the Present is dead,
Vive the Future . . .
But me, I kill the future and in the family I
destroy the love of country, courage, honor,
I am the purveyor of hell, penitentiaries,
hospitals.
Who am I finally? I am the instigator of crime
I am ruin and sorrow
I am shame
I am dishonor
I am death
I am absinthe

Each first Monday of the month, the anti-alcoholic league met at local universities to chant popular anti-alcoholic songs such as "Water of Death," "Alcohol and Liberty," "Vive la Temperance," and the exceptionally popular "L'Absinthe perd nos fils" (Absinthe loses our sons), a word play on Pernod Fils.

One of the delusions that France lived under at the time was the totally erroneous belief that the consumption of wine was not a factor in alcoholism. In fact, the anti-alcoholic movement went so far as to recommend wine as a safe and healthy alternative to other alcohols. Ironically, viticulturists and anti-alcohol groups were banding together against absinthe. On June 17, 1907 the headlines of *Le Matin* read: "TOUS POUR LE VIN CONTRE L'ABSINTHE."

Fanaticism over the Green Fairy reached such a pitch that Leon Daudet, a political reactionary and leading journalist of the day, could declare, "I am for wine and against absinthe, as I am for tradition and against revolution." In politics, those representing wine-producing regions had always been eager to get rid of absinthe as wine, now in surplus, was experiencing a price slump. Jean d'Orsay, writing in *Le Matin* (1907), commented: "To work against absinthe is to work for the starving winemakers. The deputies from the Midi know it."

J.L. Lanessan wrote in the preface to Yves Guyot's book, *L'Absinthe et le délire persécuteur* (1907): "Each of the members of Parliament would like to condemn alcoholic drinks fabricated outside their constituencies. The wine-producers only recognize the eaux-de-vie, liqueurs, and apéritifs as dangerous. The eaux-de-vie producers

would voluntarily condemn the sale of wine and beer. Each preaches for his own saint and against the demons of the other, just to the day where they believed to have found in absinthe an expiatory victim." Logic told them a nation without absinthe would drink more wine.

Politicians usually found that an anti-absinthe bill sponsored directly met overwhelming opposition; it was easier to find loopholes in existing laws. In 1900, deputy Edouard Vaillant took advantage of new debate over tax legislation to insert an amendment that would forbid the circulation and sale of any essence recognized as dangerous by the academy of medicine. It was a clever move, but unwelcomed by the government, which waited two years to ask the academy for its list. The academy managed to avoid making a clear statement by condemning *all* apéritifs because of their essences and their high alcoholic content — and suggested that such drinks should either be banned or heavily taxed. The government settled for the latter.

Georges Clemenceau's finance minister in 1906 was Joseph Caillaux, who became highly unpopular by establishing the income tax. Caillaux was a tricky operator who went on to become prime minister in 1911, to be ousted in 1912, and then to return as finance minister in 1914. Caillaux made no bones about the fact that his views on absinthe were fiscal rather than hygienic.

Caillaux listened carefully to testimony by the hygiene commission in the Chamber of Deputies on February 26, 1907 and strongly opposed the ban. Absinthe was already supporting a high tax, and a total ban would mean lost revenues of some forty million francs to the state treasury. The only thing Caillaux would agree to do was to raise the import tax on any legal essences of foreign origin that might possibly be used to make fraudulent absinthe.

Not content with taxing the drink, the temperance groups continued to call for a complete ban. Friday, June 14, 1907 marked one of the crowning moments in the anti-alcoholic crusade against absinthe. Under the auspices of *Le Matin*, 4,000 people gathered at Paris's Trocadero and demanded that the deputies and senators representing Paris and the Seine region vote to prohibit absinthe.

It was a big event with red, white, and blue banners draped everywhere. The session was opened with the national hymn sung by thousands of voices. Professor Arsène d'Arsonval, a physician and physicist (a pioneer in electrotherapy),

Why is this absinthe-drinker laughing?
The Paris daily, *Le Matin*, crusaded
against absinthe, but later apologized
to assuage liquor interests.

"What's that? Absinthe is a poison?
Drink that mominette (small absinthe)
for me and then you tell your teacher
he's a jackass!" From *Les Annales
Antialcooliques*.

In 1895, as a young minister of public education, Raymond Poincaré drafted the bill that made anti-alcoholic instruction mandatory in schools. And when he was elected president in 1913, *L'Étoile bleue* hailed him as "Le Premier Antialcooliste de France."

Georges Berry served as deputy from Paris's ninth arrondissement and fought incessantly for absinthe.

was the first speaker. "The goal of this session is to denounce before the public a national peril: absinthe and absinthisme. The utility of alcoholic drinks is beside the point: absinthe — there's the enemy!" Cheers in the crowds. Then Deputy Schmidt spoke and drew raves. There followed speeches by high authorities of science, judiciary, the army, and other representatives of the state. Jules Claretie, a historian and theater critic, declared, "Let us make the wine merchants, who have the right to live, sell wine, French wine, natural healthy wine, that which the Gascon king made to drip on the lips of his new-born. *Alors*, they've been good to France."

To end the evening, the crowd was treated to a cinematic projection of the horrors of absinthe with commentary by Dr. Maurice Letulle and Dr. Louis Jacquet. On the screen rose a series of flickering images: the absinthe drinker on the street, in the gutter, arrested by the police, taken to court, sent to an asylum, and finally immersed in the continuous bath that was the popular cure-all for the insane at that time. The finale was the fifth act of Zola's *L'Assomoir*, starring the great actor Firmin Gémier in the role of Coupeau, an alcoholic who dies in delirium tremens. (Actually, it should be noted, Zola was writing about eau-de-vie — nowhere in the novel does he specify the drink as being green in color.)

Just outside the Trocadero doors, within earshot of this fanfare, Deputy Girod from Pontarlier had managed to rouse a remarkable counter-demonstration against the anti-absinthe crowd. In fact the police had a hard time controlling the café owners and liquor merchants. Several managed to make it inside the auditorium and heckle the speakers. Just ten days later, in spite of the anti-alcoholic league's efforts, the chamber's hygiene commission met and, by a vote of eight to six, rejected banning absinthe in favor of increasing the surtax.

Part of the reason for the government's unwillingness to ban absinthe was the tremendous power wielded by the pro-alcoholic bloc. After initial gains, the temperance leagues found tough adversaries in the legislature. The Catholic National leader Georges Berry led the drink party in the chamber. Berry was a popular figure in the cafés and at the racetrack, and had Bohemian friends. One year, in a vote on the ban of absinthe, overly eager pro-drink partisans reputedly cast the votes of their absent anti-alcoholic colleagues against the proposed bill and defeated it. The following day, the alcoholic interests in Paris celebrated with a Pantagruelic feast in honor of the underhanded victory. Urban Gohier said of this: "The *mastroquet* (saloonkeeper) is the master of the Third Republic. His bar is the cornerstone of this abject government." Ernest Gordon, author of *The Anti-Alcoholic Movement in Europe*, reported that the "two thousand Paris saloonkeepers demonstrating on the Montmartre against restrictive legislation are apparently as influential in the Third Republic as the *Septembriseurs*, lunching on bread dipped in blood from the guillotine and brandy mixed with gunpowder, were in the First. They are probably more dangerous to civilization."

Barkeeps wielding political power? While London had 5,860 bars for a population of 4,536,000, Paris had 33,330 bars for only 2,601,000 people. The English counted one bar per 770 people while the French had one per 78 people. There were an estimated 477,000 drink shops throughout France, and in some villages the average was one café per ten inhabitants. In 1906, one English observer wrote: "Paris has only 17,000 bakers, 14,500 butchers, but 33,000 drinksellers. In France 160,000 employed in the production of bread; no less than 500,000 employed in cafés." Knowing this, Deputy Joseph Reinach's cynical comment that "alcohol is the literature of the people" seems less arch.

The pro-alcoholic bloc even attacked *Le Matin* after their support of the Trocadero rally. They not only silenced the paper, but readers soon found that the daily had abandoned its stand on absinthe and published an apology for the campaign! *Le Matin* said it was doing this to reaffirm its devotion to the interests of small businesses and the alcohol industry in general.

But the pro-absinthe bloc's trump card was the bottom line. No matter how many people it drove to the asylum, absinthe put fifty million francs a year into the treasury's pocket. The absinthe producers curried favor with other businesses, representing themselves as defenders of free enterprise and private property, winning the support of the Mascuraud committee, an influential business group. The economist Yves Guyot attacked the motives of the temperance movement in his book, *L'Absinthe et le délire persécuteur*.

As the anti-alcoholic movement gained ground against absinthe, wine lovers thought it prudent to stake out some safe territory. A large anti-alcoholic rally was held at the Sorbonne amphitheatre in 1914, attended by President Raymond Poincaré, who was championed by the movement. There, the famous poet and playwright, Jean

Joseph Caillaux, minister of finance, preferred to raise taxes on absinthe rather than see it banned. Caillaux later served as prime minister.

Richepin, spoke ardently: "Blessed is the French wine that we need, wine of faith, wine of love, wine of hope, wine of life. And drink it without fear, people, and drink it without remorse, but don't drink water of gold, water of fire, water of death!"

Despite the activities of the anti-alcoholic movement, the consumption of absinthe rose from 158,000 hectoliters in 1909 to 339,000 hectoliters in 1913 — a growth of 114 percent! Yet, as late as May 1914, the chamber was still refusing to raise the tax on absinthe or to ban it.

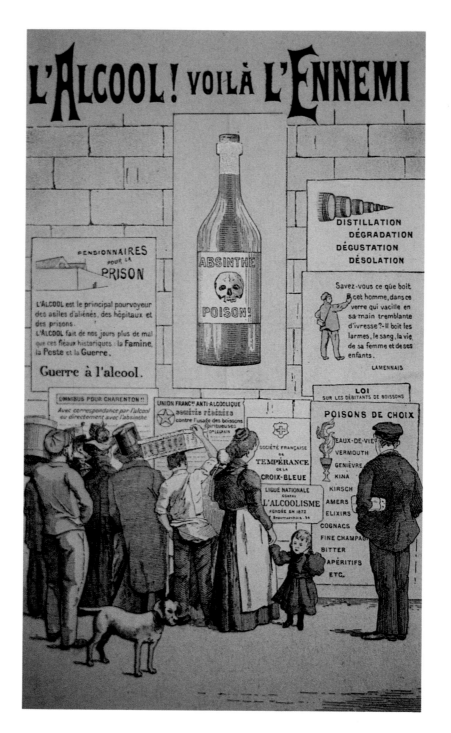

"Absinthe! Here's the Enemy!"

Chapter 10
Absinthe and War

With another Franco-German war looming on the horizon, the French looked for issues to unite their dissipated nation. Absinthe proved an excellent if unwilling sacrificial victim. Ironically, the army which had introduced absinthe to France after the Algerian war of the 1840s was now intent on destroying it.

Popular belief held that absinthe made men sterile and was, therefore, seen as a cause of France's declining birthrate. While the Germans proliferated, France had only 187 births versus 196 deaths per 10,000 inhabitants in 1911. Absinthe also was blamed for a certain moral lassitude in the face of the German military build-up. As one writer shrugged, "The absinthe drinker is content to crouch before the stalwart, honest, beer-bred Teuton." In 1907, for example, 20 percent of the French conscripts summoned to the colors were deemed physically unacceptable for duty; two decades before, the rejection rate had only been 7 percent. Statistics showed that even the chest size of the average man was smaller.

On May 3, 1900, the Ministry of War had prohibited the sale of distilled liquors in all canteens of the French army, though wine and beer — considered healthy — remained in use. By 1901, General Andrée, the minister of war, ordered that military physicians and officers give the troops systematic instruction concerning the ills of alcohol. The anti-alcoholic league was only too happy to assist, arranging lectures and temperance groups among the ranks. In the army, anti-alcoholic sections were founded, and in the barracks posters warned of the evils of absinthe, linking it with crime and syphilis. Stereopticon shows flickered in the barracks at night, and the troops were encouraged to perform anti-alcoholic skits and plays for their comrades. All were issued anti-alcoholic catechisms.

The *Bulletin Militaire*, an offshoot of the league's official organ, *L'Etoile bleue* (1911), contained excellent reports:

"The anti-absinthe group in the 122nd Regiment has decided from now on to fight all alcohols, and has joined the National League." And: "In the 133rd Regiment, twenty-one lectures on alcohol and social questions have been given in the year. The regiment boasts that it is without a drunkard." Pretty dull reading until, "In the 71st Regiment, at the temperance lecture, a hare is injected with absinthe by the regimental doctor and dies in convulsions."

Now *that* item must have made the troops think twice! An absinthe demonstration similar to

"Absinthe: It is death!"

Reactions of a guinea pig after being injected with absinthe.

the one above was reported by Captain Jacob of the 109th Infantry in his book called *Discours d'un capitaine à ses soldats*, which was honored by the French Academy. Jacob describes with perverse vividness a demonstration in which a guinea pig was injected with a quarter of a cubic centimeter of absinthe essence:

"At first it seems thunderstruck. It remains fixed in one place as if stunned. At the end of two or three minutes there follow on this stupor the most frightening agonies. Suddenly it stiffens its paws, and then makes, all at once, a prodigious leap in the air. The poor little creature, ordinarily so harmless, takes on an entirely unexpected expression of ferocity. It resembles an hydrophobic animal with its convulsed face, its twisted lips, covered with foam. In its eyes — wide open, haggard, convulsive, mad, one reads an impulse to kill."

Killer guinea pig? The description continues toward its tragicomic end: "It is now prey to hallucinations. Directly its spine curves in a half-circle. Its members and whole body are thrilled with shocks interrupted by plaintive cries. Then a brief moment of calm. The attack recommences, showing at each fresh crisis, signs of accumulated violence." The poor beast finally dies after half an hour of agony.

Maybe such lectures were essential to discipline if one is to believe a report from *Les Annales Anti-Alcooliques* (1910) which describes colonial troops stationed in Brest who amused themselves by cutting the noses off passersby with razors; naturally, the soldiers had been drinking absinthe.

The point, of course, was to keep the troops sober and to unite them against a common foe,

General Galopin (*left*) reviewing his
troops in 1915. The general banned
absinthe in Nice before the war.

"Thirty years, you hear, we've spent
thirty years to create a national drink,
and they want to suppress it!" From
Les Annales antialcooliques.

first absinthe, then the Germans if necessary. On
April 8, 1914, without waiting for the official ban
in France, French General Louis Lyautey (later
minister of war) banned absinthe from Morocco,
placed a 3,000 franc fine and a prison sentence on
anyone caught importing it, and gave merchants
just three months to export all their absinthe.
L'Étoile bleue saluted the general for the "rapid,
military execution of this enemy once as formidable as typhoid fever or rebellious tribes." The
anti-alcoholic league went on to ask if France's
602 deputies had the courage to do the same.

On June 28, 1914, Archduke Franz Ferdinand
was murdered in Sarajevo, and within a few days,
Austrians, Russians, and Serbs had begun to
mobilize. By August, war was in the air, and the
French generals had power. General Galopin, military governor of Nice, had been preparing for war
all summer. The "Boche" might be far away from
Nice, but the Italian border was nearby, Italy was
undeclared, and many of the Italians were pro-
German. It isn't easy to command hungover
troops in the hot Mediterranean sun, so Galopin
banned the use of absinthe in Nice.

Throughout the land, other generals did the
same. The feeling was that this was not just a war
of men in uniform, but a showdown between the
moral structure of two cultures. The Germans
declared war on France on August 3, 1914. In a
state of emergency, the government circumvented
democratic procedure and ordered the Prefecture

de Police to forbid all establishments to sell absinthe and similar drinks. On August 16, the minister of the interior, Louis Malvy, forbade the sale
of absinthe nationwide and even outlawed drinks
similar to absinthe.

Le Rappel, the venerable democratic mouth-
piece, crowed over the victory: "The genius and
blood of our race have been saved from the fatal
brink of lunacy and degeneracy." On the strength
of the preliminary victory over absinthe, the
Chamber of Deputies voted 422 to 58 on March 4,
1915 to ban the production, circulation, and sale
of absinthe in France. The law went into effect on
March 16, 1915.

As the factories shut down, one of the few
voices in the chamber to oppose the decision was
Monsieur Adolphe Girod, deputy of Pontarlier.
Girod continued with the argument he had
espoused all along — that high-class absinthes
such as Pernod were not the villains, that the real
problem lay in cheap imitations of the drink which
flooded the market. But the din of war over-
whelmed his pleas.

Incredibly, after decades as the national drink,
"Absinthe has been expulsed from France just like
a dumb Boche," wrote Leon Bailby in *L'Intransigeant.* A street organ, *Ruys Blas,* ran an article
entitled, "Funeral Prayer for Absinthe," suggesting that, "The poets who sang of the 'consoling
fairy' will have to find other more worthy subjects
to strum their lyres to. Drunkenness shouldn't be

The Absinthe Gillet company used this
clock to promote their product.

an excuse for anything. The unfortunate who
looks to forget sorrow in drink is a lost man:
sorrow passes, but drunkenness remains."

One hears in this not only a reprimand to poets
such as Verlaine and Rimbaud, who wallowed in
the gutter of decadence, but also a challenge to the
French people to overcome indulgence, self-pity,
and moral weakness if they were to survive as a
nation.

One of the big differences between banning
absinthe in Switzerland and France was that the
Swiss made it a popular movement in peacetime
and the French ban was primarily an emergency
war measure. In Switzerland, the right of the state
to intervene in a dangerous industry had not been
contested in a long time. After the ban in Switzerland, the government indemnified the absinthe
industry quite fairly.

Francis Carco wrote in his Montmartre
memoirs: "Absinthe has always
accentuated certain traits of the
capricious temperament, of dignity, of
obstinacy, of buffoonery, particularly
in women." Watercolor by an anonymous artist.

Symbols of a fading era.

An absinthe drinker in the street paper,
Le Frou-Frou, 1906.

France, however, had seen several cases of state intervention in private industry, and there was a history of compensation for expropriation of property and goods. In 1902, for example, France had prohibited the sale of saccharine because it hurt the sugar industry, and it had banned wine made from dried raisins as it hurt the wine industry. It also had nationalized production of white phosphorus and was making a profit off it, which bothered a few people. But in all cases, the government had indemnified private enterprise.

Following the intense anti-absinthe campaign, there was still a strong feeling that the absinthe distillers such as Pernod were "greedy poisoners" who had profited by pouring this terrible green curse down the throats of millions of innocent Frenchmen. Many believed these companies were rich and needed no indemnity. The socialists,

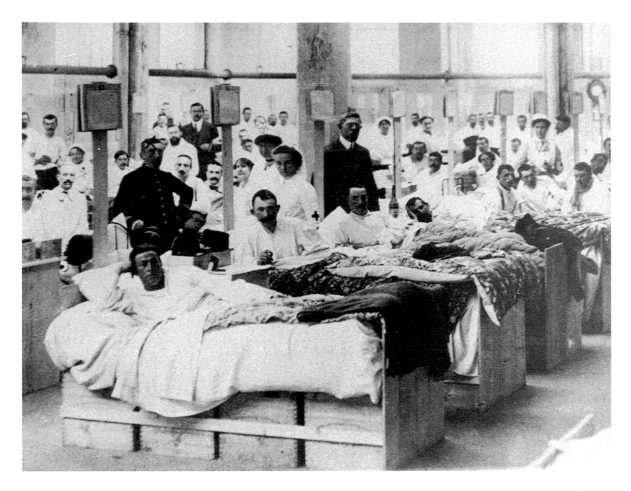

The Pernod factory at Pontarlier
served as a field hospital during the
Great War. The beds are made of
stacked absinthe crates.

collectivists, and others hostile to private enterprise were so vocal that the minister of labor felt
compelled to declare that "this is unacceptable, in
a democratic society all men have a right to justice,
the rich, the millionaires as well."

Two weeks after the official ban, a government
committee was formed to supervise compensation
of wormwood cultivators. The farmers were indemnified for each crop-load they delivered, and
one million kilos of dried herbs were burned. No
money, however, was allocated for loss of future
revenues.

The distillers were badly treated. Despite the
zealous lobbying of Adolphe Girod, the absinthe
distillers were never reimbursed for their own
inventory of dried wormwood plants. Their three
million liters of distilled absinthe were requisi-
tioned, and they were paid only the base price.

Many of the factories just shut down. Thousands
were put out of work in the Doubs region, but of
course many of the men were already fighting in
the trenches or decomposing in graves.

Demonstrations were staged to protest giving
twenty-three million francs to "public poisoners,"
but as the war escalated, tragedy and suffering
soon drew focus away from the drink eulogized
by decadent poets. One million, three hundred
and fifty-three thousand Frenchmen died in the
trenches. Absinthe was soon just one of many
victims of a war that would change France and
Europe forever.

The famous Absinthe Robette poster by
Privat-Livemond, 1896.

Chapter 11
After the Ban

Paris was a different city after the Great War. Another generation was taking over the boulevards, a generation which traveled by Monsieur Peugeot's motorcars instead of carriages, a generation which painted cubist aeroplanes instead of impressionist picnics, a generation which drank American cocktails instead of absinthe. As Robert Burnand wrote:

"The spirit of the boulevard is dead, because its old halls are gone whose acoustics gave the least remark a wonderful sonority. It was killed by the haste, the hustle and the bustle. Where will one find again the time to stroll, to daydream, to chisel a thought, to launch an arrow? As paradoxical as it may seem, it was killed by the invasion of industrial drink. Absinthe, the magical absinthe of the green hour, whose jade flower blossomed on every terrace — absinthe poisoned the Parisian in a delicious way, at least giving him fertile imaginings, whereas the other cocktails sickened one without exaltation."

During the war, the Pernod plant at Pontarlier had served as a field hospital. The ban on absinthe crippled Pernod Fils, and on December 31, 1917, the Société Veil-Picard & Compagnie sold the plant after 110 years of operation to Nestlé, the chocolate concern. Within a few years, most of Pontarlier's twenty-two distilleries had closed.

Even after the war, the question of indemnities for absinthe producers remained alive in the Chamber of Deputies. As late as 1925, Adolph Girod, venerable representative of Pontarlier, proposed a law that would allow the distillers to get rid of their stockpiled absinthe by selling it abroad to French colonies or countries where no French troops were stationed. But the government decided it was not worth "poisoning" others to rid France of a problem.

The lack of absinthe left certain elements in France searching for a replacement. As early as 1911, the chemist Louis Pillet had proposed a solution that would satisfy both health fanatics and the pro-alcohol bloc, a "safe" absinthe made without wormwood. "I add that this adaptation will maintain the resources of the treasury and won't oblige the factories to close," suggested the chemist. But it was 1922 before the French government passed a bill allowing the sale of imitation (wormwood-free) absinthe.

Drinks similar to absinthe tried to recall the pre-war days, promoting the same ritual involving the water fountain, sugar cubes, and trowel-

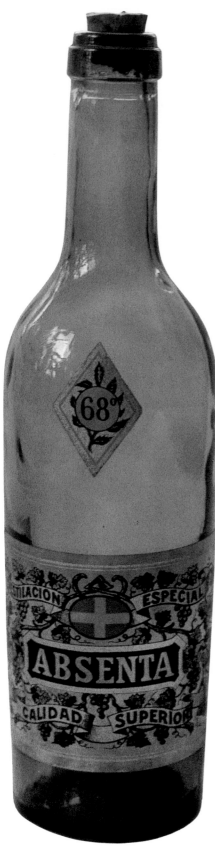

Absenta, a Spanish brand of absinthe, has never been outlawed in Spain.

The two absinthe spoons in the center are shaped like the Eiffel Tower.

shaped spoon. But it was never quite the same. The general public's desire for real absinthe was gone.

The Veil-Picard brothers were determined to keep the Pernod Fils brand name alive, and they contacted André Hemard who had successfully converted his company in Montreuil-sous-Bois to produce an anise-flavored drink called Amourette, which was made from herbal wines. In July 1926, the two firms merged under the name Maisons A. Hemard et Pernod Fils Réunies.

In 1938, the legal alcohol content of apéritifs was raised to 45 percent along with a larger allowable amount of aromatic essences. Pernod did well until the Second World War when, under German occupation, the law of August 23, 1940 banned spirit-based apéritifs. The company then developed a wine-based apéritif called first Vin Pernod, later known as Perkino, and a non-alcoholic drink called PSA (Pernod Sans Alcool).

In 1959, the company changed its name to Pernod S.A., and in 1965, it merged with the venerable Distillerie Suze, which produces a bittersweet apéritif made from the gentian plant. (Picasso, incidentally, did a cubist collage of a Suze bottle.)

Absinthe's departure had little effect in France and its demise was a pyrrhic victory for the anti-alcoholic movement. After the war, the temperance movement in France never regained its former strength or fervor. American Prohibition (1920–1933) was in effect, but it was hardly a success.

The minute the 1915 ban passed, a black market for absinthe was created. All during the war one bought it in the oddest places, from farmers who bootlegged it in stills hidden in their cowbarns to the corner barber who would slip you a bottle of "hair tonic."

The Bohemians still gathered in the Parisian cafés, but instead of the green muse, the artists and boulevardiers sipped whiskey and even martinis. "Our epoch," wrote the painter Kees Van Dongen, "is the cocktail epoch. Cocktails! They are all colors. They contain something of everything. No, I do not merely mean the cocktails that one drinks. They are symbolic of the rest." The decadent languor was replaced by nostalgia or headlong modernism. Ether, opium, or hashish competed with American cocktails.

After the ban of absinthe in France, Pernod Fils opened an absinthe plant in Tarragona, Spain in 1918. As a young journalist in the 1920s, Ernest Hemingway discovered absinthe when he went down to Spain to see his first bullfights. In *The Sun Also Rises* (1927) Hemingway records a morosely funny scene between Jake Barnes, the narrator, and Bill at the end of the fiesta in Pamplona. Robert Cohn has left for Paris, and Lady Brett has run off with the bullfighter chap:

> "What's the matter? Feel low?"
> "Low as hell."
> "Have another absinthe. Here, waiter! Another absinthe for this señor."
> "I feel like hell," I said.
> "Drink that," said Bill. "Drink it slow."
> It was beginning to get dark. The fiesta was going on. I began to feel drunk but I did not feel any better.
> "How do you feel?"
> "I feel like hell."
> "Have another?"
> "It won't do any good."
> "Try it. You can't tell; maybe this is the one that gets it. Hey, waiter! Another absinthe for this señor!"

Hemingway liked absinthe enough to keep a few bottles on hand when he moved from Paris to Key West, Florida. Absinthe was illegal in America, of course, but anything was available in the renegade town of Key West. Most likely, this absinthe was acquired in Cuba, just ninety miles away, where Hemingway often went marlin

fishing and later acquired a house. In 1931, Hemingway wrote a letter to a journalist friend, Guy Hickok: "Got tight last night on absinthe and did knife tricks. Great success shooting the knife underhand into the piano. The woodworms are so bad and eat hell out of all furniture that you can always claim the woodworms did it."

Hemingway must have seen humor in the transposition of woodworms and wormwood, though it is doubtful that his second wife, Pauline, appreciated his treatment of the furniture.

Later, in *Death in the Afternoon*, Hemingway used absinthe to explain why he gave up bullfighting: "My decision was reached on a consideration of my physical ineptitudes, on the welcome advice of my friends and from the fact that it became increasingly harder as I grew older to enter the ring happily except after drinking three or four absinthes which, while they inflamed my courage, slightly distorted my reflexes."

Hemingway returned to Spain for the Spanish Civil War and again drank absinthe. In the novel, *For Whom the Bell Tolls*, Robert Jordan, holed up in a cave with Republican guerrillas, pulls out a canteen filled with absinthe purchased in Madrid and hands it to a suspicious gypsy:

"It was milky yellow now with the water and he hoped the gypsy would not take more than a swallow. There was very little of it left and one cup of it took the place of the evening papers, of all the old evenings in cafés, of all the chestnut trees that would be in bloom now in this month, of the great slow horses of the outer boulevards, of book shops, of kiosques, and of galleries, of the Parc Montsouris, of the Stade Buffalo, and of the Butte Chaumont, of the Guaranty Trust Company and the Ile de la Cité, of Foyot's old hotel, and of being able to read and relax in the evening; of all the things he had enjoyed and forgotten and that came back to him when he tasted that opaque, bitter, tongue-numbing, brain-warming, stomach-warming, idea-changing liquid alchemy. "

In London, absinthe was considered a sign of French decadence, but it was never outlawed and enjoyed a vogue among the avant-garde and the upper class. Even after the ban in France, absinthe found its way to London, imported from Holland, Spain, and France. Though the total imported from these countries (legally) was only 14,428 gallons from 1921 to 1930, it was enough to raise a few eyebrows. Dr. C.W.J. Brasher wrote with concern in *The Lancet*, on April 26, 1930: "I have been informed by a member of an exclusive London club that when a cocktail is ordered it is

Legendary American expatriates drinking absinthe before the bullfights in Pamplona, Spain, 1926 (*left to right*): artist Gerald and Sara Murphy, Pauline Pfeiffer (soon to be the second Mrs. Hemingway), Ernest Hemingway in Basque beret, and his wife Hadley. Three Spanish shoeshine boys attend Gerald. Hemingway loved absinthe for its "idea-changing" effect.

customary to inquire whether a 'spot' shall be added — that 'spot' being absinthe."

But George Saintsbury, professor of English and French literature at the University of Edinburgh, came to absinthe's defense in his treatise on wines and spirits, *Notes for a Cellar-Book* (1920). Saintsbury described absinthe as a drink which "burns like a torchlight procession . . . the extraordinary combination of the refreshingness and comforting character in odor and flavor." Saintsbury, with his civilized passion for absinthe, claimed that "only a lunatic" would drink it neat, and his own moderation kept him going to the age of eighty-eight.

In Evelyn Waugh's first novel, *Decline and Fall*, Margot Beste-Chetwynde, the deceptively demure proprietress of an international chain of whorehouses, gazes into the opalescent depths of her absinthe frappé as she contemplates snaring a husband. Waugh himself drank absinthe and vodka as a hangover cure when he was up at Oxford where his crowd of aesthetes held Wilde's memories dear.

Alec Waugh, Evelyn's brother, drank absinthe in the Domino Room at the Café Royal in London and reported that for him the drink had the curious property of doubling the effect of every drink that was taken after it, so that half a bottle of wine with the meal that followed would feel the equivalent of a whole bottle. "I took it with appropriate reverence," wrote Alec Waugh, "in memory of Dowson and Arthur Symons, Verlaine, Toulouse-Lautrec, and the Nouvelle-Athènes. I only drank it once for I loathed the taste of it. In those days you ordered a dry martini 'with a dash,' a dry martini was half gin and half vermouth and a dash was not Angostura bitters but absinthe. Even thus diluted I thought it ruined the cocktail. But I daresay I should like it now."

When Somerset Maugham visited San Francisco in the thirties, his host, the elegant stockbroker Bertram Alanson, would roll out the red carpet. Before dinner, Maugham and the Alansons would be served caviar, champagne, and martinis laced with absinthe, of which Bertram had a steady supply from a mysterious source. Maugham himself was no stranger to absinthe, but he was never a habitué.

Raymond Chandler, that transplanted Englishman, found a way to mix absinthe into his sardonic view of Los Angeles. In *Farewell My Lovely*, Chandler's narrator, Marlowe, visits the house of a perfumed male client and comments: "It was a nice room, if you didn't get rough. . . . It was the kind of room where people sit with their feet in their laps and sip absinthe through lumps of sugar and talk in high, affected voices and sometimes just squeak. It was a room where anything could happen except work."

The last great absinthe drinker in Paris was the American millionaire poet Harry Crosby who was so obsessed by Wilde's *The Picture of Dorian Gray* that he installed a plaque of marble in the Hotel d'Alsace in Paris where Wilde died and toasted the Englishman from a silver flask of absinthe.

Like Hemingway, Crosby served as a driver in the American Ambulance Corps during World War I. In 1917, the nineteen-year-old St. Mark's graduate was driving an ambulance at Verdun when it received a direct hit that totally destroyed the vehicle, gravely injured a fellow driver, but left Harry miraculously unharmed. Most people would consider this a lucky stroke, but for Harry it was a revelation. At the time, he described his battle experiences as "the ride through red explo-

Oxford don George Saintsbury said only a "lunatic" would drink absinthe straight. Portrait by Sir William Nicholson.

Somerset Maugham drank absinthe in San Francisco in the thirties.

Harry Crosby, an American born with a silver (absinthe) spoon in his mouth, lived recklessly in Paris.

sions and the violent metamorphose from boy into man." Malcolm Cowley, who wrote about Harry in the last chapter of *Exiles Return*, saw it differently. "There was indeed a violent metamorphosis but not from boy into man; rather it was from life into death." Harry never got over the trauma and could never shake the intoxicating intimacy of death.

Harry Crosby was the quintessential American expatriate in Paris during the twenties, and yet he was unlike any of the others, according to Geoffrey Wolff in his brilliant Crosby biography, *Black Sun* (1977). While most of the American writers and artists in Paris came from the middle class and lived on tight budgets, Harry was from a wealthy Boston family of Grews and Van Rensselaers, while his uncle and godfather was none other than J. Pierpont Morgan, Jr. Bohemianism did not attract Harry, and he considered himself an aristocrat. His favorite bar was the Ritz, his dark suits were impeccable (morbidly accented with an artificial black carnation), and he owned racehorses. When he did step out of bounds, it was not to picturesque Bohemia but to the extremities of sex and drugs.

Most American writers in Paris spent their time almost exclusively with other Americans (Fitzgerald for example, never learned to speak French properly); and they wrote about America, a country to which they intended to return. Harry Crosby rejected American culture and embraced the French wholeheartedly. He worshipped Rimbaud and hated Boston with a passion.

While Crosby's hedonism made him notorious, he was also developing a reputation as a poet and publisher. His Black Sun Press published some of the greatest writers of his time: James Joyce, D.H. Lawrence, Ernest Hemingway, Hart Crane (whom Harry introduced to absinthe), Archibald MacLeish, Kay Boyle, and Aldous Huxley. These were also his party guests, though for most of Harry's parties, another kind of guest was more appropriate.

Harry had many vices — so many that absinthe, from a medical standpoint, had little effect on his health. But Harry loved absinthe. He loved what it did to him, and he loved what it stood for — the days of Wilde, Rimbaud, Baudelaire. His diaries, later published as *Shadows of the Sun* (1977), are filled with references to absinthe, cocaine, opium, and hashish.

Crosby and his wife Caresse were famous for their raucous parties and naturally kept a good

Harry and Caresse Crosby with their dog, Clytoris, at Le Bourget airport, 1928.

stock of drugs and absinthe on hand for guests. Where they obtained their supply is rarely stated in the diaries, but Crosby recorded on May 5, 1927 that he met Caresse at the Gare du Nord, "and she comes running down the platform carrying two ponderous volumes of Aubrey Beardsley and two bottles of Absinthe."

In July that summer, Crosby drove down to the mountains of Spain for the running of the bulls at Pamplona. Arriving in the evening, he found the bullfight was postponed because of rain and went drinking in Hotel La Perla: "One absinthe two absinthes three absinthes and I said goodnight and wandered the streets (wet and dark) and someone located Number 30 . . . and there were six women selling for five pesetas each and thirty men clamoring and I did not stay."

The next day, Crosby woke up to a large breakfast of "eggs and beer cold in tall glasses (later on cold absinthe in tall glasses) and Hemingway of the Sun Also Rises drove past in a carriage and shouted at us and Waldo Pierce was with him looking like Walt Whitman and everyone began rushing off for the bullfight (one last round of absinthe) and there was a young bootblack kneeling at someone's feet shining and singing and everyone forgot about the absinthe and the bullfight and he sang weird . . . half-Spanish half-African songs."

At the Crosbys' apartment at 19 Rue de Lilas or at their renovated mill on the property of Count Armand de la Rochefoucauld (one of Caresse's lovers), their guests could dabble in just about everything. "A great drinking of cocktails in our

Caresse Crosby, photographed the
day Harry killed himself.

bathroom — it was too cold in the other rooms . . .
and there were eleven of us all drinking and
shrieking and we went to eat oysters and then to
the Jungle where there was a great drinking of
whiskey and mad music and life is exciting nowa-
days with all the pederasts and the lesbians — no
one knows who is flirting with who."

Harry loved books more than anything. When
his cousin, Walter Berry, gentleman, man of letters, and longtime lover of Edith Wharton, died,
Harry inherited several thousand volumes. He
sold most of them except books by Rimbaud
whom he always worshipped. But when he went
to a bookshop on June 12, 1928 books were not
what he was after. He recorded in his diary: "I
went and procured in a bookshop a bottle of very
old absinthe (it was a choice between this or an
erotic book with pictures of girls making love) and
the man in the bookshop recommended Ramuz Le
Guerison de Maladies but as I already had the
Guerison to all Maladies i.e. the absinthe I did not
buy the book but went instead to an apothecary's
where I bought two empty bottles marked hair
tonic into which I decanted the absinthe one bottle
on each hip and down the hill to the station where
I sat in the sun and drank beer and read Endymion
until the train for Paris arrived." (Guerison means
"cure" in French.)

Harry suffered from terrible nightmares and
symbolically killed himself by shooting a pistol at
his portrait and at his poems. His suicidal nature is
revealed in the last lines of his poem "Assassin":

> I shall cut out my heart take it into my
> joined hands and walk towards the Sun
> without stopping until I fall down dead.

Harry actually believed that he and Caresse
were deities of the sun. In Egypt, he had a giant
sun tattooed on his back, spoke of the Egyptian
sun god Ra, and lay for hours in the sun burning
his body to the golden brown of an Aztec. He had
sun princesses too, beautiful girls he would meet at
parties and with just a few words and the intensity
of his personality, whisk away to the Ritz bar and
then to some darkened room. It was always for
love that he had sex, but he fell in love so quickly.
Like most of the great seducers, he felt he had
unlimited amounts of love to give away. Harry
had once copied a line from Oscar Wilde in his
notebook: "The only way to get rid of a temptation is to yield to it."

As affairs undermined their marriage, Harry and Caresse slipped from their mythical orbits, and Harry spun off alone, flying closer and closer to the sun. Inspired by Lindbergh, he took flying lessons and felt freedom in leaving the earth. He was becoming Icarus. On Armistice Day 1929, Harry soloed for the first time. But, as this last diary entry, written in New York on December 9, 1929, reveals, the thrill of flying wasn't enough:

One is not in love unless one desires to
die with one's beloved

There is only one happiness
    it is to love and be loved

On December 10, Harry was meant to meet Caresse and his mother for tea at J.P. Morgan's and then to take them to dinner and the theater with Hart Crane. Instead, in a borrowed apartment in the Hotel des Artistes off Central Park West, Harry and one of his mistresses, Josephine Rotch Bigelow, took off their shoes and lay on the bed together, fully clothed.

The day before, Josephine had sent Harry an impassioned poem which ended with the words, "Death is *our* marriage." Mrs. Bigelow, twenty-two years old, was married to the son of one of Boston's most proper families. She was beautiful and resembled Harry so much they might have been brother and sister. At last Harry had found someone who believed in death. Now, lying on the bed, he pressed a .25 caliber Belgian automatic pistol to Josephine's left temple and pulled the trigger. For two hours Harry lay beside her, feeling the sun die around him. Then he put the pistol to his own forehead.

Harry's pilot's license arrived at his home in France after he killed himself. It is in the Crosby archives; there are no flight entries on it. In a sense, his whole life had been a frenzied flight without a manual. Ezra Pound wrote, "Crosby's life was a religious manifestation. His death was . . . a death from excess vitality. A vote of confidence in the Cosmos."

For Crosby, the drink that had charmed Wilde, Lautrec, Rimbaud, and the other pre-War dandies and artists, was worth an ocean of associations, a morbid green paradise. But in the end, absinthe, a sacrament of a bygone age, was not enough for him.

Josephine Rotch Bigelow, Harry's lover and partner in death.

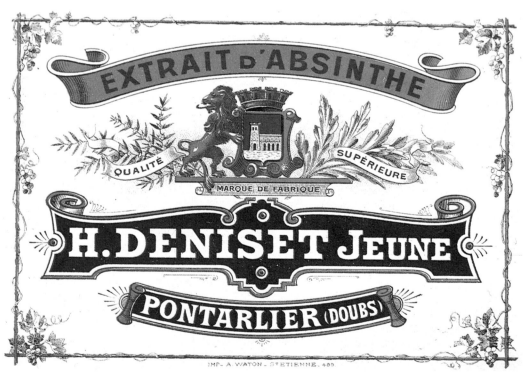

Vintage absinthe labels.

Chapter 12

Absinthe Today:
Vive La Fée Verte!

In 1981, the Swiss government invited French President François Mitterrand to a dinner at the Hôtel DuPeyrou in Neuchâtel, a town at the eastern end of the Val-de-Travers, the valley where Dr. Ordinaire, the sisters Henriod, and the Pernod family first made absinthe. In honor of the visit, Mitterrand's host served a *soufflé glacé à la Fée Verte* for dessert. Television cameras roamed the room, as the word "absinthe" was chuckled mischievously into the microphones. It was an evening to remember.

So was the morning after, when Swiss liqueur authorities cornered the restaurateur Daniel Aimone to inquire about the dessert. Aimone stated there was no presence of the precious liquid on his premises, and none was found after the six inspectors and policemen spent two days going through all 4,000 wine and liquor bottles in his cellar. That did not stop the Swiss. If it was proved that the dessert contained the real thing, Monsieur Aimone risked a fine of 200 Swiss francs. But if it turned out that the restaurateur used legal pastis instead of absinthe, they would charge him with fraud. Aimone finally admitted to the latter — and still became a culinary folk hero.

Why the big fuss? Because the Val-de-Travers has had a thriving community of absinthe bootleggers for almost eighty years. Just two weeks before Mitterrand's visit, two big distillers had been brought to trial. The press had fun with the Mitterrand affair.

When absinthe was legal, that is before 1907, there had been virtually no bootleg absinthe in Switzerland. The minute the ban fell, clandestine distillers went to work, generally working on a small scale as a way to get their families through hard times. For many years, the Régie fédérale des alcools (liquor authorities) knew the addresses of all the buyers of alcohol, usually pharmacists, but averted their eyes. Distillers boldly printed up their own labels for La Fée Verte. A discreet inquiry at a café for *la bleue* or *un midi moins dix* ("the blue" and "a ten to noon," slang for absinthe), and you could walk away with a bottle for forty Swiss francs.

Articles repeatedly appeared in the Swiss newspapers with nostalgic references to the Val-de-Travers's favorite beverage, often poking fun at the stuffed shirts of the Régie fédérale. As George Droz, septuagenarian author, newspaper correspondent, and longtime fan of absinthe, wrote in 1979, "To make absinthe in the Val-de-Travers is the demonstration of a certain state of the spirit, rebellious and independent, proud and unsinkable, that characterizes the people here."

  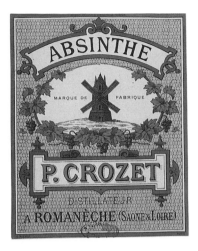

Vintage absinthe labels.

In 1960, pressured by the powers that be, the Régie fédérale suddenly went into action, and a team of inspectors and police arrested seventy distillers in the Val-de-Travers. Georges Droz felt the crackdown came when people stopped making absinthe for just pocket money and made thousands of liters. "And some of the absinthe being made wasn't even very good — it was just macerated, not distilled," Droz added.

In August 1983, a man who bought thousands of gallons of cut-rate industrial alcohol from an Italian supplier was condemned to nine months in jail and a fine of 80,000 Swiss francs. Furthermore, he was liable for customs and state taxes amounting to some 1,888,203 Swiss francs! Even to the Swiss, this was excessive. He is now paying fifty Swiss francs a month until the year 4980. (Yes, 4980.)

While writing this book, I realized I needed real absinthe. Two weeks later, I paid a visit to the land of the Green Fairy. Pontarlier lies in the region known as the Franche-Comté near the Swiss border. It was early December, and snow already dusted the Jura Mountains and its foothills as I stepped off the high-speed train from Paris. I rented a car at the station and took a spin around town. Of the town's twenty-two absinthe distilleries, only two remain, producing anise-flavored drinks on a small scale. The old Pernod factory is now the site of the Nestlé chocolate factory.

In the Pontarlier Museum, the director, Joël Guiraud, has devoted two rooms to absinthe's past. A young, dark-bearded man originally from Burgundy, Guiraud greeted me enthusiastically and led me through the exhibit of posters bearing the names of Pernod, Pernot, and Duval — some of whose descendants still live in Pontarlier. Gui-

Another Charles Maire still life with
absinthe and Pontarlier newspaper.

The physiological effects of absinthe were described in the *American Journal of Pharmacy* (1868): "You seem to lose your feet, and you mount a boundless realm without horizon. You probably imagine that you are going in the direction of the infinite, whereas you are simply drifting into the incoherent."

Woodley Herber's "Original Anise Flavored Absinthe" appeared in American "head-shops" in the 1970s.

raud let me smell the bags of dried wormwood and explained how the beautiful copper distilling apparatus had once worked. He gave me vintage absinthe bottle labels and photocopies of articles about absinthe. It was all very interesting, but somehow lifeless. I still wanted the real thing.

From Monsieur Guiraud I learned that Roland Vuillemin, the mayor of Pontarlier who was also a deputy in the National Assembly, was lobbying in Paris to resurrect absinthe in France. The reasoning went as follows: In 1992, Spain becomes a full-fledged member of the European Economic Community; Spain is the only country in Europe where absinthe is still legal; will Spain be able to sell absinthe in other countries, and if so, why shouldn't France be able to do the same? When I asked Guiraud where I could find real absinthe, he looked at me strangely but suggested I try in the Val-de-Travers, across the border in Switzerland.

When I braked at the border, the guards eyed my rented Peugeot with little interest and waved me on to the Swiss guardhouse. I was counting on the same easy reception on my return trip. Because, with any luck, I was about to become an absinthe-runner.

I drove up over the pass in the Montagnes de Larmont, passed through a tunnel, and descended into the beautiful Val-de-Travers. On my right was the source of the Areuse River, which runs northeast up the valley to Neuchâtel. The valley, fifty miles long, was no more than three miles across, and the sheltering, pine-forested hills were mantled with snow. Driving by barns — one of which I recognized as an ancient drying shed for absinthe — I thought of the fields under the snow, fields that had once grown pungent acres of wormwood in summer, and I remembered Rimbaud's description of absinthe, "that sagebrush of the glaciers."

Twenty minutes later, I pulled into Couvet, the hamlet where Dr. Ordinaire first promoted the elixir. The town spread on either side of the Areuse River. There was a good church and several pretty houses in the traditional Swiss style, but the dominant feature of the town was a factory emblazoned with the name "Dubied." A century ago that would have meant absinthe — it was Major Dubied who bought the recipe from Mère Henriod — but today Dubied is a company that produces knitting machinery. In fact, the factory is a sore point with the townsfolk, because due to bad management and bankruptcy, it is laying-off employees.

I discreetly asked a few townsmen for leads on a

The Val-de-Travers, where modern absinthe was invented. Today, clandestine Swiss distillers produce thousands of gallons of bootlegged absinthe for local consumption.

bottle of absinthe, but the answer was always no. One old fellow shook his head and advised, "Better to let the past be the past."

I drove to nearby Môtiers, and from a café I called a man named Pierre-André Delachaux at his house. Shortly after the Mitterrand affair, Pierre-André Delachaux, then head of the Neuchâtel *conseil* and later a socialist deputy from the region, was accused of contributing two bottles of absinthe to prepare a soufflé glacé eaten by 450 people, among them important officials of the Neuchâtel region. By Swiss law, it is not illegal to drink absinthe, but it is illegal to distill, sell, or transport it. Delachaux was snagged because he had transported his two bottles fifty meters on a public road. His trial was marked with "hilarity," as one paper put it, and he was let off with a light fine, eighty francs. Today, he is director of the Musée des Mascarons in Môtiers.

Fifteen minutes later, Delachaux drove his minibus up to the museum. Tall, bearded, and balding, he might have been a handsomer version of Verlaine. We went into the museum and up the stairs to the two rooms he has dedicated to the Green Fairy. As in the Pontarlier museum, the objects were arranged to give the impression of a nineteenth-century bistrot: on the bar stood a glass water fountain with spigots poised over four absinthe glasses.

On one table stood a full bottle of vintage absinthe bearing the label Deniset — real pre-1910 absinthe with the leaded seal unbroken — almost within my reach! Delachaux picked up a twenty-five liter wooden barrel and pulled the cork out.

"Here, smell this," he said. I put my nose to the hole and inhaled the heady aroma of absinthe, part anise, part ambrosia.

"Do you know where I can get some real stuff?" I asked.

Delachaux's smile faded. "I don't give out addresses," he said ratherly sharply, but he gave me an old absinthe spoon and some ideas for literary research.

Ten minutes later, I was on the road again. It was dark when I reached the town of Fleurier and found the dilapidated Hotel de la Poste. Opening the door, I found a dimly lit bar and restaurant occupied by a dozen locals. An Alain Delon police film played on a television. The locals stopped talking and all watched me enter.

I drank a beer at the bar, looked this group over, trying to decide who I would ask about absinthe. I finally lost courage, put on my coat and hat, and went out for a walk. It was cold and clear outside. I walked down to the train station and watched the last train come and go. My absinthe quest was beginning to seem futile.

It was after nine when, halfway back to my hotel, I passed an épicerie with the lights still on. The shopkeeper was working late, trying to install a new venetian blind in his front window. As he tried to hammer in a nail, one side of the shade would slip, and he had to start over again. The little bell tinkled as I opened the door. "Need some help putting that thing up?"

The shopkeeper was about my age, mid-thirties, long-faced with dark hair and a beard. He smiled. In a few minutes, working together, we finished the job. He pulled the shade up and down twice, until he was satisfied it worked. He offered me a beer.

His name was Henri. Originally from Lausanne, he had moved here ten years ago with his wife and two children to get away from the big city. He dabbled in health food, raised bees, and studied Zen. In the first few minutes, I felt confident enough to tell him about my project. "Do you know anyone who makes absinthe?"

"Sure," he laughed. "Just about everybody in this *town* makes it — except me!"

Henri told me about an old lady who made fine absinthe. "Nice old biddy, a widow, just trying to get by, you know. She's been busted once already though, so I don't know how she'd react to being interviewed . . . but I'll get you a bottle, don't worry. Check in with me tomorrow."

I couldn't believe my luck. We shook hands warmly, and I went back to the Hotel de la Poste.

The next day, I stopped by Henri's. "Any news about, the, er, 'product'?" I asked.

"Yeah, but it's not good. The old lady is scared to meet anyone, particularly a journalist. Don't worry, I'll get you a bottle."

I spent the day driving around the countryside, killing time. The next morning, I drove up to Henri's shop. There were customers inside, and I stood out as a stranger. While Henri sliced cheese and packed eggs, I feigned intense interest in the display of local honey on the shelves. When the shop was clear, I looked hopefully at Henri, but he shook his head. "Bad news. I tried to get the old lady once more, but she really didn't want to meet anyone."

My heart sank. "Can't we get a bottle of absinthe from someone else?"

He looked at me blankly and then smiled. "Hey, relax. I've already got the bottle — I was just trying to get you an interview as well."

In the backroom, he pulled a tall unmarked green bottle from a burlap sack. "Voilà, La Fée Verte." He pulled the cork and held the bottle up to my nose. The aroma was not dangerous or degenerate or depressing as the history of absinthe would lead one to believe — no, it smelled like bottled summer. In my racing imagination, contraband absinthe was one of the wonders of the world. Henri sold it to me at cost, forty Swiss francs, we shook hands warmly, and I left for the border.

The Swiss guards had paid little attention to me when I entered Switzerland. Now, to my alarm, three guards came out of the guardhouse. One examined my passport and asked the nature of my business here. Had I made any purchase? Sweaters or watches perhaps? They wanted the keys to my trunk. But all they found was my overnight bag and two jars of honey. The absinthe bottle was stashed under the hood, strapped into the tire jack holder. A moment later, they waved me through, and I drove into France.

My apartment, on the Left Bank of Paris, overlooks the Seine and the Tuileries beyond. To the left, is the Musée de la Légion d'honneur; directly ahead in the distance stands Sacré-Coeur atop Montmartre; and to my right is the grand facade of the Musée d'Orsay. Built as a train station in 1900, the building is now a museum of the nineteenth century and holds that icon of absinthophilia, Degas's *L'Absinthe*.

One evening this winter, at l'heure verte when the mist of Paris was just settling over Sacré-Coeur, I knew it was time to open the bottle of contraband absinthe. For the sake of ritual, I put some music by Erik Satie, another absinthe drinker, on the cassette player. On the table before me stood a tall heavy absinthe glass I had purchased in the Paris flea market. Its bottom was scratched from the hundreds of times absinthe drinkers had stirred the last bits of sugar with the trowel-shaped spoons. But when I poured two inches of the pale emerald liquor into the glass, the scratches disappeared. I marveled at the color, my nose drew in the fragrance. From a box, I took an absinthe spoon given to me by a Parisian biologist and absinthe expert, Marie-Claude Delahaye. I balanced the spoon on the rim of the glass and thought of Picasso's *Glass of Absinthe* of 1914. As I slowly poured water over the sugar cube and it dripped down into the absinthe, the glass turned milky green, then opalescent, just as all the poets had written. I felt as much anticipation as I had on my first communion in church.

It had a light minty, licorice taste that was slightly antiseptic but refreshing. I drank it easily and it was soon gone. I poured another and listened to the music of Satie. I had a little notebook next to me, intending to record my impressions of absinthe as Aldous Huxley did for drugs in *Doors of Perception*. But absinthe was nothing like hard drugs. It was a gentle thing. The music played and I mixed another absinthe. I wrote a letter to a friend in New York, then to a friend doing time in a French prison. From time to time, I looked out at the lights of Paris as night fell. I had been in Paris for six years, and I was leaving as soon as I finished my book. I thought of the things I had done in Paris, and the things I had not done. I always wanted to swim across the Seine on a summer night, even though a few years ago a drunken German tried this and drowned. My novel was still unfinished, I'd broken up with a woman, and my mother had just died. I suddenly wished I had invited a friend to share this drink with me — next time. I drank another absinthe and began doodling in a notebook. I would be too moved to say how I felt. It was just Paris and my own life passing. But it wasn't bad. I felt it impossible to recapture time in words, and I gave up trying, just letting my eyes follow the lights of a barge moving slowly up the Seine. I filled the glass again.

In the morning, I did not remember much of the night before until I had swallowed a coffee downstairs at Le Rapide. Then it came to me that at some point in the previous evening, I thought I knew the answer to life; only now I had forgotten it.

It was a long, hard winter, but by spring the absinthe bottle, which I shared with friends, was empty. Then one day a package arrived from a friend, Martin Muller, a Swiss art dealer living in San Francisco. Inside was a *demi-bouteille* of absinthe with a note: "Don't ask me how I got this, but drink it with pleasure." Instead, since my absinthe time was over, I kept it sealed as a talisman.

It seems appropriate to end this book with words written during the true absinthe era. In 1899, Rainer Maria Rilke wrote about absinthe and a Czech poet named Machal:

"For awhile the poet gazed silently into his glass of absinthe and replied softly and dolefully: 'Spring is here.'

"All expected something else to follow but the poet again seemed to be on the way to the pallid garden of his dreams. He saw his glass of absinthe grow and grow until he felt himself in the center of its opal light, weightless, completely dissolved in this strange atmosphere."

Appendix

A Modern Analysis of Absinthe

Even after its official demise, absinthe continues to fascinate modern science. Naturally, the focus is on wormwood and its essence, thujone. In 1963, German scientists Gildemeister and Hoffman proved that thujone was identical to the tanecetone of tansy and the salvanol of sage. Other pharmacologists have traced wormwood's history in mythobotany. For the most part, these studies classify the thujones as a convulsant poison. But until recently, few have been able to answer questions about how absinthe actually works on the brain and what it made users feel.

The drug culture of the late 1960s prompted studies on marijuana and heavier recreational chemicals. American scientists J. del Castillo, M. Anderson, and G.M. Rubottom (*Nature* Magazine, January 31, 1975) observed similarities between the psychological effects attributed to absinthe and those of marijuana *(Cannabis sativa)*. Their chemical analysis of thujone and of the active chemical in cannabis, THC (tetrahydrocannabinol), shows that the similarity is not just a coincidence.

Thujone, they say, has traditionally been grouped with two $C_{10}H_{16}O$ isomers, camphor and menthol, and has been classified as a convulsant poison. "The molecular geometry of these three compounds is so different, however, that it is difficult to believe that, at low doses, they interact specifically with the same pharmacological receptors. At large doses, it is always possible that they exert similar, less specific actions by virtue of common physiochemical properties."

They also note that both thujone and THC are terpenoids and have a similar molecular geometry and similar functional groups available for metabolism (in humans). This close geometrical relationship is illustrated in Figure 1, where the bonds common to both molecules have been accentuated in bold. The absinthophile chemist may appreciate their explanation more than the poet will:

"The similarities include the gem-dimethyl groups at C_8, the C_7 methyl groups, the bonds connecting carbons 8,4,3,2 and 1 of THC and 8,5,4,3 and 2 of thujone, the *a* hydrogen at C_4 in THC and the cyclopropyl 5-6 bond of thujone and the 4-5 bond in THC and the 1-5 bond in thujone. Finally, although there is no direct correspondence between the oxygen of the thujone molecule and the hydroxyl group of THC, it seems possible that both react with a common site of a pharmacological receptor such as that indicated by X in Fig. 1, without changing the orientation or relative position of either molecule."

Del Castillo and his colleagues further demonstrated that "these oxygen atoms are likely to be the principal pharmacological binding sites" because the primary metabolites are products of oxidation. And these metabolites have been suggested as the actual psychotomimetic agents in marijuana. Because thujone contains an allylic group similar to that in THC, "both systems should be available for similar oxidative reactions." This means that "both thujone and THC exert their psychotomimetic effects by interacting with a common receptor in the central nervous system."

In 1979, Craig Pyes, a writer for that peculiar American journal of indulgence, *High Times*, conducted a thorough, sympathetic investigation into absinthe's toxicity. He found most studies indicated that absinthol (the oil derived from wormwood) and its drug thujone ($C_{10}H_{16}O$) were highly powerful. Dr. Samuel M. Pollack, a Harvard-trained chemist who had formerly supervised Schenley's production of Absant, said, "Thujone is definitely toxic. It is classified as a poison. Before the U.S. approves of any liquor formula, it must be almost 100 percent thujone free."

But Dr. Richard Rappolt, executive editor of *Clinical Toxicology*, reported in 1979: "Our feeling has been, as far as medical toxicology is concerned that the most harmful ingredient in absinthe is not wormwood or thujone, but ethanol, which is drinking alcohol. What most people object to in absinthe is mostly the name 'wormwood.' It makes them think that little maggots are eating their brains. But there is little known about absinthe."

The Food and Drug Administration (FDA) only puts a substance on a "Generally Regarded as Safe" list if laboratory studies on its lifetime effect on two kinds of animals can establish a permissible "no effect" level (the quantity at which the substance can be ingested without injury to brain, liver, or fetus). Since animals are not humans, the human "no-effect" level is required to be 100 times lower than it is for animals.

Experiments established a generally accepted measure for thujone poisoning as thirty milligrams of thujone for each kilogram of a rat's body weight. At this level, thujone causes mild convulsions and lesions of the cerebral cortex in the rat's brain. The maximum non-lethal dose (administered orally) is seventy-five milligrams per kilogram. Though thujone is psychoactive in relatively

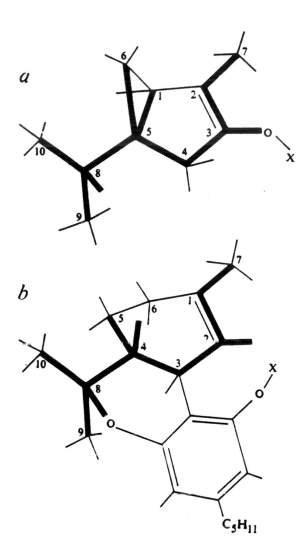

Figure 1. The molecular structures of thujone-enol *(a)* and THC *(b)*. Bonds common to both molecules are drawn in bold lines. An X indicates the site of the receptor with which the oxygen of the thujone molecule or the hydroxyl group of the THC molecule may react.

low dosages, it is not positive that it causes cumulative damage to the nervous system.

Pyes deduced that the intake of thujone in one ounce of traditional absinthe (drunk by a 150-pound man) is fifty times *less toxic* than the dosage required to cause a minimum toxic reaction in humans, leaving a safety margin of fifty, half of what would be necessary to qualify by FDA standards.

This equation, corroborated by three toxicologists, indicated to Pyes that it was doubtful whether anyone — even over long periods of drinking — could swallow enough commercially bottled absinthe to suffer from anything other than alcoholic poisoning. For example, an ounce of absinthe contains much less thujone than is contained in the amount of wormwood oil once frequently prescribed by doctors for alleviation of fever. On that day in 1905 when Jean Lanfray murdered his family, he had consumed thirty times less thujone than it would take to make a rat shudder. Yet Lanfray had consumed enough liters of wine and brandies to overload his system with alcohol.

The effect of a drink is determined by two factors: the amount of alcohol and the substances it is delivered with. In genuine absinthe, there are usually thirty to thirty-five drops of absinthol in a quart, and the average glassful contains considerably less than two full drops. Absinthe had one of the highest percentages of alcohol of any liquor made — at least any legal liquor — and had such a small percentage of solid matter in solution as to make comparison with any other liquor out of the question.

As recently as 1979, the French scientist Millet and his colleagues analyzed anise and several other ingredients in absinthe. Although anise was not really toxic, they noted that, "A strong dose provokes drunkenness, trembling, epileptic convulsions, then like opium, muscle spasms, analgesia and sleep, all the characteristics of stupifiers." Progressive doses of essence of hyssop were injected into Wistar rats whose brains were monitored with an electrocorticogram. The results confirmed earlier studies that essence of hyssop has a convulsive property. Millet's conclusion was that *all* the essences in absinthe were dangerous and had epileptic properties, particularly hyssop which could cause "cumulative damage."

So we are left wondering if absinthe — or rather the wormwood in absinthe — is as bad as everyone thought. For the time being, no definitive conclusion seems possible.

Michael Montagne and Donald Vogt noted in 1981, "The nature and meaning of the absinthe experience are still not clear . . . With the flurry of 'legal highs' that are being discovered by the subculture, does absinthe have the potential for being rediscovered and used? . . . Though absinthe may appear to be only a nineteenth-century phenomenon, it may have twentieth-century implications."

The following is a chemical abstract of thujone by mythobotanist, Michael Albert-Puleo:

"Thujone, a terpene-like ketone, is termed 3 thujamone or 3 sabinone in IUPAC nomenclature. Absinthol, tanacetone, and salviol are terms which have been applied to the thujone extracted from *Artemisia absinthium*, *Tanacetum vulgare*, and *Salvia officinalis*, respectively. Thujone is a colorless oil with the following physical constants: B.p. = 199-200 C.: M.W. = 152.23: Specific Gravity = 0.915-0.919 at C. It is soluble in alcohol, ether, and chloroform, and insoluble in water.

"The odor of thujone is said to resemble that of menthol. It is isomeric with camphor, another CNS stimulant, although its chemical structure is rather unlike camphor. Thujone can be isolated from the natural oils with bisulphate, or via fractional distillation and crystalization, and has been synthesized by man.

"In nature, thujone exists as two forms, levoratory *a*-thujone and dextrorotatory *b*-thujone, the former occurring in thuja and sage, the latter in tansy and wormwood. The work of Short and Read has shown that *a*-thujone and *b*-thujone are in fact mixtures of the diastereoisomers l-thujone and d-isothujone in dynamic equilibrium."

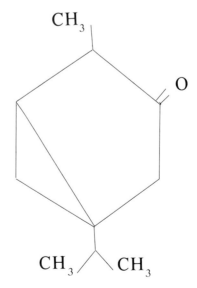

Figure 2. Molecular structure of thujone.

Bibliography

I began research for this book in 1979 at the New York Public Library. I later found material in Paris at the Musée d'Orsay, the Académie de Médecine, and at the Centre Nationale pour la Défense Contre l'Alcoolisme which has period journals such as *Les Annales anti-alcooliques* and *L'Étoile bleue* and hard-to-find books like Edmond Couleru's *Au Pays de l'Absinthe.* Most of the circa 1900 newspaper items are quoted as they appeared in other texts, such as Marie-Claude Delahaye's informative *Absinthe: Histoire de la Fée Verte.* I found material in recent French newspapers such as *L'Indépendant, Le Monde,* and *La Voix du Haut-Doubs,* and in Swiss newspapers such as *La Gazette de Lausanne, Le Matin, Le Courrier du Val de Travers,* and *F.A.N-L'Express.* I also found material in Marie-France Briselance's contemporary series in *Initiative,* Pernod's in-house magazine, and in old Pernod Fils promotional pamphlets. The Balesta material came from Ronald K. Siegel and Ada E. Hirschman's article in *Social Pharmacology.* Ronald Pickvance's article in *Apollo* was essential for the chapter on Degas. Patricia E. Prestwich's article aided my chapter on politics. Roger Shattuck's wonderful book, *The Banquet Years,* was an inspiration for the chapter on Jarry.

Adriani, Götz. *Toulouse-Lautrec.* London: Thames and Hudson, 1987.

Albert-Puleo, Michael. "Mythobotany, Pharmacology, and Chemistry of Thujone-containing Plants and Derivatives." *Economic Botany* (The New York Botanical Gardens) 32 (January–March 1978): 65–74.

Balesta, Henri. *Absinthe et Absintheurs.* Paris: Marpon, 1860.

Barr, Alfred H. *Picasso: Fifty Years of His Art.* New York: Arno Press for The Museum of Modern Art, 1980.

Baudelaire, Charles. *Art in Paris 1845–1862.* Translated and edited by Jonathan Mayne. Oxford: Phaidon Press, 1965.

———. *Flowers of Evil.* New York: New Directions Books, 1955.

———. *Les Paradis artificiels.* Edited by Claude Pichois. Paris: Club du Meilleur Livre, 1961.

Bernard, Oliver, ed. and trans. *Arthur Rimbaud, Collected Poems.* Harmondsworth, Middlesex, England: Penguin Books, 1962; Penguin Classics, 1986.

Bernier, Georges. *Paris Cafés, Their Role in the Birth of Modern Art.* New York: Wildenstein & Co., 1985.

Bett, W.R. "Vincent Van Gogh (1853–90), artist and addict." *British Journal of Addiction* (London) 51 (1954): 7–14.

Blocher, E., and H. Steck. "Cinquante ans d'interdiction de l'absinthe." *Cahiers complémentaires de la question de l'alcool en Suisse.* Cahier no. 31. Basel: Benno-Schwabe & Co., 1958.

Brasher, C.W.J., M.D. "Absinthe and Absinthe Drinking in England." *The Lancet,* (London), April 26, 1930.

Burchell, S.C. *Imperial Masquerade: The Paris of Napoleon III.* New York: Atheneum, 1971.

Burnand, Robert. *Paris 1900.* Paris: Librairie Hachette, 1951.

Cadeac, C., and A. Meunier. "Nouvelles notes sur l'étude physiologique de la liqueur d'absinthe." *Comptes Rendus de la Société de Biologie,* no. 41 (1889): 213–15.

———. *Recherches expérimentales sur les essences: Contribution a l'étude de l'alcoolisme.* Paris: Asselin et Houzeau, 1892.

Carco, François. *Montmartre à Vingt Ans.* Paris: Albin-Michel, 1938.

Castillo, J. del, M. Anderson, and G.M. Rubottom. "Marijuana, absinthe and the central nervous system." *Nature,* no. 253 (1975): 365–66.

Cazals, F.-A., and Gustave LeRouge. *Les Derniers Jours de Paul Verlaine.* Paris: Mercure de France, 1923.

Chauveau, Paul. *Alfred Jarry.* Paris: 1932.

Coolus, Romain. "Souvenirs sur Toulouse-Lautrec." *L'Amour de l'Art,* April 1931.

Cooper, Douglas. *Henri de Toulouse-Lautrec.* New York: Harry N. Abrams, 1982.

Corelli, Marie. *Wormwood: A Drama of Paris.* 3 vols. London: Richard Bentley & Son, 1890.

Couleru, Edmond. *Au Pays de l'absinthe — Y est-on plus criminel qu'ailleurs ou moins sain de corps et d'esprit? — Un peu de statistique, s.v.p.* Montbéliard, France: Société Anonyme d'Imprimerie Montbéliardaise, 1908.

Cowley, Malcolm. *Exiles Return.* New York: Viking Compass Edition, 1956.

Crosby, Harry. *Shadows of the Sun, The Diaries of Harry Crosby.* Edited by Edward Germain. Santa Barbara, Calif.: Black Sparrow Press, 1977.

DeCroos, Pierre. *La Réglementation légale de l'absinthe.* Paris: Imp. H. d'Homont, 1911.

Delahaye, Marie-Claude. *L'Absinthe, Histoire de la Fée Verte.* Paris: Berger-Levrault, 1983.

Droz, Georges. *Feu . . . L'absinthe.* Moutier, Switzerland: Éditions de la Prévôté, 1973.

Ellmann, Richard. *Oscar Wilde.* London: Hamish Hamilton, 1987.

Emboden, William A. "Absinthe, Absintheurs, and Absinthism, A Brief History of Wormwood." *Terra,* (The Natural History Museum of Los Angeles County) 21, no. 4 (Spring 1983).

Flower, D. and H. Maas. *The Letters of Ernest Dowson.* London: Cassell and Co., 1967.

Fothergill, John. *My Three Inns.* London: Chatto & Windus, 1921.

Girod, Adolphe. *Proposition de loi tendant à autoriser l'écoulement des stock d'absinthe*. Paris: Chambre des députés, 1925.

Goncourt, Edmond and Jules de. *Journal, mémoires de la vie littéraire*. 22 vols. Monaco: Éditions Robert Ricatte, 1956–58.

Guyot, Yves. *L'absinthe et le délire persécuteur*. Paris: 1907.

Hemingway, Ernest. *Death in the Afternoon*. New York: Charles Scribner's Sons, 1932.

———. *For Whom the Bell Tolls*. New York: Charles Scribner's Sons, 1940.

———. *The Sun Also Rises*. New York: Charles Scribner's Sons, 1926.

Hercod, R. "The Prohibition of Absinthe in Switzerland," *International* (London) 4 (1908): 18–22.

Hoog, Michel. *Gauguin, Life and Work*. New York: Rizzoli International Publications, 1987.

Hugh, H.P. "The Two Montmartres." *Paris Magazine,* June 1899.

Hulsker, Jan. *The Complete Van Gogh*. New York: Harrison House/Harry N. Abrams, 1984.

Laborde, J.-V. "Rapport au nom de la commission de l'alcoolisme sur les boissons spiritueuses, apéritifs et leurs essences et produits composant les plus dangereux." *Bulletin de l'Académie de Médecine*, no. 48, (1902): 685–712.

Lee, Thomas Courtney, M.D. "Van Gogh's Vision: Digitalis Intoxication?" *The Journal of the American Medical Association,* 245, no. 7 (February 20, 1981): 657–88, 727–29.

Legrain, Pierre. *Absinthe et Absinthisme*. Conférence faite à Neufchâtel, Lausanne, 1903.

Le Pichon, Yann. *Gauguin: Life, Art, Inspiration*. New York: Harry N. Abrams, 1987.

Littlewood, Ian. *Paris: A Literary Companion*. London: John Murray, 1987.

London, Jack. *John Barleycorn*. Santa Cruz, Calif.: Western Tanager Press, 1981.

Longaker, Mark, ed. *The Stories of Ernest Dowson*. New York: A.S. Barnes and Company, A Perpetua Book, 1960.

McMullen, Roy. *Degas: His Life, Times and Work*. Boston: Houghton Mifflin Company, 1984.

Magnan, Valentin. "Alcoolisme aigu: épilepsie causée par l'absinthe. Alcoolisme chronique: accidents épileptiformes, symptomatiques des lésions organiques." *Comptes Rendus de l'Académie des Sciences,* no. 73 (1871): 341–42.

———. *De l'Alcoolisme; des divers formes du délire alcoolique et de leur traitement*. Paris: Adrien Delahaye, 1874.

———. *Étude expérimentale et clinique sur l'alcoolisme*. Paris: Renou & Maulde, 1871.

Marcé, M. "Sur l'action toxique de l'essence d'absinthe." *Comptes Rendus de l'Académie des Sciences,* no. 58 (January–June 1864): 628.

Millet, Y., P. Tognetti, M. Lavaire-Pierlouisi, M.D., Steinmetz, J. Arditti, and J. Jouglard. "Étude de la toxicité d'huiles essentielles végétales du commerce: essence d'hysope et de sauge." *Médecine Légale,* 23, no. 1 (1980): 9–20.

Montagne, Michael, and Donald D. Vogt. "Absinthe: Behind the Green Mask." *The International Journal of the Addictions* 17, no. 6 (1982): 1015–29.

Morgan, Ted. *Maugham: A Biography*. New York: Simon & Schuster, 1980.

Motet, M. *Considérations génerales sur l'alcoolisme et plus particulièrement des effets toxiques produits sur l'homme par la liqueur d'absinthe*. Paris: Thèse de Paris, 1859.

Panouillé, Jean-Pierre. "Et les français prirent goût à l'absinthe!" *L'Histoire,* no. 52 (January 1983): 50–59.

Petitfils, Pierre. *Rimbaud*. Translated by Alan Sheridan. Charlottesville: University Press of Virginia, 1987.

———. *Verlaine*. Paris: Compagnie Française de Librairie, Le Spectacle du Monde, 1981.

Pickvance, Ronald. "L'Absinthe in England." *Apollo* 77 (May 15, 1963): 395–96.

Ponchon, Raoul. *La Muse au cabaret*. Paris: Fasquelle, 1920.

Poulet, Georges. *Baudelaire: The Artist and His World*. Geneva: Éditions d'Art Albert Skira, 1981.

Prestwich, Patricia E. "Temperance in France: The Curious Case of Absinthe." *Historical Reflections/Réflexions historiques* (Canada) 6, no. 2 (Winter 1979).

Rachilde [Mme. Marguerite Vallette]. *Alfred Jarry, The Supermale of Letters*. Translated by Ralph Gladstone and Barbara Wright with introduction by Barbara Wright. New York: New Directions Books, 1977.

Redman, Alvin, ed. *The Wit and Humor of Oscar Wilde*. New York: Dover Publications, 1959.

Richardson, Joanna. *The Bohemians: La Vie Boheme in Paris 1830–1914*. Cranbury, N.J.: A.S. Barnes, 1971.

———. *Verlaine*. New York: Viking Press, 1971.

———. *La Vie Parisienne 1852–1870*. New York: Viking Press, 1971.

Roubinovitch, Jacques. "Les Alcools qui tuent." *Le Matin* (brochure). Paris, 1907.

Rubin, William, ed. *Pablo Picasso: A Retrospective*. New York, The Museum of Modern Art, 1980.

Saintsbury, George. *Notes on a Cellar-Book*. London: MacMillan London, 1978.

Schneider, Pierre. *The World of Manet 1832–1883*. New York: Time-Life Books, 1968.

Seigel, Jerrold. *Bohemian Paris: Culture, Politics, and the Boundaries of Bourgeois Life, 1830–1930*. New York: Penguin Books, Elisabeth Sifton Books, 1987.

Sévigné, Madame de. *Lettres*. 14 vols. Paris: L. Hachette et Cie., 1868.

Shattuck, Roger. *The Banquet Years*. New York: Vintage Books, 1968.

Sherard, R.H.. *My Friends the French*. London: T. Werner Laurie, 1909.

———. *My Twenty Years in Paris*. London: Hutchinson, 1905.

Siegel, Ronald K., and Ada E. Hirshman. "Absinthe and the Socialization of Abuse: A Historical Note and Translation." *Social Pharmacology* 1, no. 1 (1987): 1–12.

Starkie, Enid. *Arthur Rimbaud*. New York: New Directions Books, 1968.

Turner, H.E. "The Shaky Case against Absinthe." *American Mercury,* March 1937.

Van Gogh, Vincent. *The Complete Letters of Vincent Van Gogh, with Reproductions of all the Drawings in the Correspondence*. Greenwich, Conn.: New York Graphic Society, 1959.

Varenne, E., and L. Godefroy. *Étude sur l'Absinthe (Spiritueux Absinthe), Sa Fabrication, Sa Constitution, Son Usage*. Paris: 1903.

Vogt, Donald D. "Absinthium: a nineteenth century drug of abuse." *Journal of Ethnopharmacology* 4 (1981): 337–42.

Waugh, Alec. *In Praise of Wine and Certain Noble Spirits*. New York: W. Sloane Associates, 1959.

Weber, Eugen. *France: Fin de Siècle*. Cambridge: Harvard University Press, Belknap Press, 1986.

Wertenbaker, Lael. *The World of Picasso*. New York: Time-Life Books, 1974.

Wolff, Geoffrey. *Black Sun: The Brief Transit and Violent Eclipse of Harry Crosby*. New York: Random House, 1976.

Zolotow, Maurice. "Absinthe." *Playboy,* June 1971, 169–74.

Picture Credits

Index